Praise for

BECOMING THE BELOVED DISCIPLE

In *Becoming the Beloved Disciple*, Eric Huntsman gives us a sustained reading of The Gospel of John as a handbook of Christian discipleship. John shows us the different paths that people take as they come to a testimony of the Savior. Some experience miracles, while others believe doctrines, and others still experience an immediate and overwhelming spiritual witness of the Messiah. Huntsman teaches us that, while all of these paths are different, they all lead to Jesus Christ—and nobody knows enough to judge another person's spiritual journey. This is a remarkable and urgently necessary book.

—MICHAEL AUSTIN, vice president for academic affairs and provost, University of Evansville; author of *Re-reading Job: Understanding the Ancient World's Greatest Poem*

Throughout Eric Huntsman's resonant work thrums a graceful and irresistible invitation to more truly love the Savior and all that are His. In a day of increasingly global and therefore diverse Church membership, such a message is not only timely but also vital. Lending scholarly meticulousness and interpretive precision the softest compassionate embrace, Huntsman urges each of us—faithful, faith-wanting, faith-waning—to see ourselves and others and all our varied spiritual journeys in the template of the Beloved Disciple. I've closed these pages inspired to come, follow, and believe.

—MELISSA DALTON-BRADFORD, author of *Global Mom: A Memoir* and *On Loss and Living Onward*, cofounder of two global nonprofits: one refugee-related and the other dedicated to women's civic engagement

Becoming the Beloved Disciple is a powerfully insightful book that will not only increase understanding of the stories contained in the Gospel of John, but will also invite each of us to become a beloved disciple of Jesus Christ as we learn from the example of the Apostle who first carried that name. Using examples from both scriptural stories and personal accounts, Eric Huntsman invites each reader to examine their own journey closer to Christ and shares insight on how each of us has the potential to become beloved. It is a brilliant concept that opened my heart to consider the word "beloved" with an entirely different perspective.

—EMILY BELLE FREEMAN, popular Latter-day Saint speaker and author of *Even This, Getting to the Place Where You Can Trust God with Anything*

Becoming the Beloved Disciple is written by one who is both a disciple of the Savior and one of the Church's finest New Testament scholars. Eric D. Huntsman knows what and of Whom he writes. The doctrines Brother Huntsman discusses and the practices he describes will help the reader better understand how to come unto Christ and receive His mercy and grace. Saints, sinners, and the rest of us in between will all be blessed by studying this instructive and edifying publication.

—DANIEL K JUDD, professor of ancient scripture and interim dean of religious education at Brigham Young University

This is nothing short of a landmark study of the Gospel of John written for members of The Church of Jesus Christ of Latter-day Saints. Huntsman draws on his mastery of biblical Greek, the best of Johannine scholarship, and relevant church sources to deliver a remarkably rich set of reflections and insights into the Fourth Gospel. In addition to the book being both highly educational and spiritually edifying, Huntsman deploys his well-honed teaching and speaking skills to produce a volume that is an engaging page-turner. In *Becoming the Beloved Disciple*, Huntsman is firing on all cylinders. It may be his finest work yet.

—GRANT UNDERWOOD, Richard L. Evans Chair of Religious Understanding, Brigham Young Universtiy

In his latest study of the gospel of Jesus Christ, Eric Huntsman identifies two "vital questions for believers in every age." They are, according to Huntsman, How can we truly know Jesus? and How can we better follow Him? Huntsman correctly opines, "This is what discipleship, anciently and today, is all about." Anyone interested in how to become a more committed, faithful, and consecrated disciple of Jesus Christ will find *Becoming the Beloved Disciple: Coming unto Christ through the Gospel of John* helpful. Huntsman carefully uses the characters found in the gospel of John and inspired insights from modern leaders of the Church of Jesus Christ to highlight important lessons about discipleship. Although readers will learn more about John's gospel on every page, the most important result of a careful study of this book is the possibility of their finding themselves an integral part of the story as they desire to be a follower of Christ worthy to be called "beloved disciples."

—RICHARD NEITZEL HOLZAPFEL, professor emeritus of religious education at Brigham Young University

The growing diversity within the twenty-first-century Church is both a gift and a challenge. This timely, wise, and compassionate book embraces that diversity and affirms that energetic and meaningful discipleship is Jesus's open invitation to each of God's children, regardless of race, ethnicity, gender, sexuality, or ideology. Combining a scholar's mind, teacher's skill, and disciple's devotion, Eric Huntsman brings alive the Gospel of John as a guidebook for following Christ in our modern age.

—PATRICK Q. MASON, Howard W. Hunter Chair of Mormon Studies at Claremont Graduate University and author of *Planted: Belief and Belonging in an Age of Doubt*

Also by

ERIC D. HUNTSMAN

God So Loved the World: The Final Days of the Savior's Life

Good Tidings of Great Joy: An Advent Celebration of the Savior's Birth

The Miracles of Jesus

Worship: Adding Depth to Your Devotion

COAUTHORED AND EDITED

Jesus Christ and the World of the New Testament (with Holzapfel and Wayment)

The Ministry of Peter, the Chief Apostle (coeditor)

Thou Art the Christ, The Son of the Living God: The Person and Work of Jesus in the New Testament (lead editor)

Becoming the Beloved Disciple

Coming unto Christ through the Gospel of John

Eric D. Huntsman, PhD

CFI
An imprint of Cedar Fort, Inc.
Springville, Utah

discipulis meis per omnes annos
quos docui, qui me semper docent

To all my students through the years,
Whom I have taught and who always teach me.

ISBN 13: 978-1-4621-4601-7

Published by CFI, an imprint of Cedar Fort, Inc.
2373 W. 700 S., Springville, UT 84663
Distributed by Cedar Fort, Inc., www.cedarfort.com

Library of Congress Control Number for the hardback edition: 2018959621

Cover design by Jeff Harvey
Cover design © 2018 Cedar Fort, Inc.
Edited by Kathryn Watkins and Nicole Terry
Typeset by Kaitlin Barwick

Printed in the United States of America

10 9 8 7 6 5 4 3 2 1

Printed on acid-free paper

Contents

ACKNOWLEDGMENTS

During the fall semester of my sophomore year at Brigham Young University, I took an intensive honors course titled, "Greek through the New Testament." Taught by C. Wilfred Griggs, it taught us the basics of Classical Greek and took us through the Gospel of John, beginning what has been a career-long affair with the Fourth Gospel. I am indebted to Wilfred and other teachers, especially the late R. Douglas Phillips and my friend John F. Hall, III, for what they taught me about language, history, and, most of all, scripture and the gospel.

I am grateful to my publisher, Cedar Fort Publishing and Media, for having confidence in this project and hastening its production. I wish to particularly thank Kathryn Watkins, Kaitlin Barwick, and Nicole Terry for their professionalism and attention to detail. I also owe a great debt to my longtime former assistants, Stephen Betts and Julia Min-tsu Chiou, who helped with the early research and who provided immeasurable help with their careful proofing and perceptive insights. Finally, my current assistants, Jacob Inman and Grace Hendricks-Bingham, have provided yeoman service in source checking and collection in the final weeks of our work.

For many years my family and close friends have heard me constantly speak about the Gospel of John. In this last year they have been supportive and constantly encouraged me to press forward in the face of obstacles to this book's publication. Among this number I especially recognize my friend, Daniel K Judd, interim dean of religious education at Brigham Young University. As always, I express my love and appreciation to my wife, Elaine.

This book is dedicated to my students—past, present, and future—whose eagerness to learn and love of the gospel have invigorated and inspired me.

Above all, I offer my thanks and adoration to Almighty God and to my Lord, Jesus Christ. The greatest desire of my life is to be found his true disciple.

FOREWORD

By Michael Austin

Several years ago, at the Catholic university where I worked, I attended a lecture by Father Greg Boyle, a Catholic priest who has spent much of his life ministering to gang members in Los Angeles. When his presentation was over, Father Boyle spent about a half an hour answering questions from the audience. I only remember one of the questions, which was, "Why don't you teach these young men to be good Christians and worship Jesus?" I will never forget the answer. He said simply, "Jesus wants disciples; he doesn't need a fan club."

This was a pivotal moment in my own spiritual development as a member of The Church of Jesus Christ of Latter-day Saints. It is the first time that I thought seriously about "discipleship" as something distinct from followership, believership, or membership in a religious organization. Religious fandom propels us to proclaim our devotion loudly, to defend our faith in the public square, and to use our religion as an excuse to exclude and despise others. Discipleship, on the other hand, calls us to something higher—to emulate our Savior and to do everything we can to see other people through His eyes. The word for this in the Christian tradition is "charity."

It was not long after hearing Father Boyle speak that I encountered the work of Eric Huntsman, an outstanding thinker from my own faith tradition who writes as both a learned scholar and a committed disciple of Jesus Christ. These are not easy identities to reconcile. Scholarship and discipleship require different skills, different inclinations, and, very often, different temperaments. Most of us who try to combine them find it impossible to do so consistently. We end up sacrificing the conventions of one for the expectations of the other. No one can serve two masters.

Throughout his career, however, Huntsman has managed to combine these identities admirably into books about Christ's life and mission, marrying biblical exposition with devotional writing, often weaving in personal narratives and his reflections in the process. In his new book, he follows the same path to create a marvelous book that is about discipleship itself. *Becoming the Beloved Disciple* is an extended meditation on the Gospel of St. John—a meditation with depth and substance, that combines great faith and first-rate scholarship to provide an example of how we can interact with John to become better disciples.

As Huntsman presents it, the main concern of the Gospel of John, after its powerful presentation of Jesus as the divine Son of God, is to define the nature of Christian discipleship—and to do so in a way that is charitable and inclusive. In episode after episode, John shows us the different ways that people develop testimonies of Christ: the first apostles, the mother of Jesus, Mary Magdalene, Nicodemus, the Woman at the Well, the family of Lazarus, and even Thomas, who doubted, and Peter, who denied knowing the Christ.

All of these figures are converted to Christ, but none of them take the same path. Some of them believe immediately, while others believe only after coming through a period of doubt and disbelief. Some experience miracles, others feel the overwhelming call of divine love, and others still must find their way clear to assent intellectually to the reality of the Messiah. All of the roads are different, but they all lead to the same destination: a life of discipleship and an eternity of faithful service and infinite progression. Every one of these figures—and each of us—becomes the Beloved Disciple when they arrive at the fundamental tenets of Christian discipleship: a personal, loving relationship with Jesus Christ, a witness that he died on the cross for us, and hope in the resurrection.

The different characters in John don't show us "the way"; they show us that there are many ways to get to that same destination. And that is Huntsman's most important point. His analysis of John recognizes the many roads that people take on their spiritual journeys. One can easily imagine somebody writing a different sort of book with the same title and subject matter. Such a book might use all of the same stories "but focus on their similarities rather than their differences to produce a 'one-size fits all' model, which might reflect the author's path more than the path modeled by Jesus himself."

There are plenty of books that take this approach, and plenty of lists of how one is supposed to follow Jesus. But Huntsman rejects this approach in favor of a more open and inclusive understanding of how one becomes a disciple of Jesus Christ that is clearly anchored in the text itself and in harmony with what we know of the gospel from other sources Acknowledging the many different kinds of spiritual journeys is itself an act of discipleship. Huntsman reads text, not just with clarity, but also with charity—by which I meant that he sees people's individual spiritual paths the way Christ sees them. He understands how much Christ loves all of us who are trying to find a way to Him, even when that way is bumpy and full of obstacles—and even when it goes through darkness, denial, and doubt.

In *Becoming the Beloved Disciple*, Huntsman gives us a sustained reading of the Gospel of John as a handbook of Christian discipleship. John shows us the different paths that people take as they come to a testimony of the Savior. Some experience miracles, while others believe doctrines, and other still experience an immediate and overwhelming spiritual witness of the Messiah. Huntsman teaches us that, while all of these paths are different, they all lead to Jesus Christ—and nobody knows enough to judge another person's spiritual journey. This is a remarkable and urgently necessary book.

Michael Austin
Evansville, Indiana
September 2018

PREFACE

John 17:3 teaches, "And this is life eternal, that they might know thee the only true God, and Jesus Christ, whom thou hast sent." Two vital questions for believers in every age are, How can we truly know Jesus? and, How can we better follow him? This is what discipleship, anciently and today, is all about. The accounts of Jesus's mortal ministry and his first followers in the New Testament provide familiar stories of how people came to know Jesus and strove to follow him, sometimes faithfully and sometimes with mixed success. Of the four Gospels, John uniquely highlights the theme of discipleship, focusing not only on the Twelve but also on believers of all backgrounds and stations.

The Gospel of John powerfully portrays Jesus as the divine Son of God; contains many stories and thought-provoking symbols not found in the other Gospels; and paints intriguing, relatable portraits of characters with whom we can identify, thus providing us instructive models of discipleship. Nephi taught that we should liken all scriptures to ourselves (1 Nephi 19:23), and the characters in John provide a wonderful and accessible way of doing this. They come to, accept, and follow Jesus each in his or her own way, and then bring others to him just as we do. At a time when the Church and society-at-large are grappling with questions of unity and diversity, the characters of John show that there are many ways to be disciples of Jesus Christ. Yet there are some fundamental beliefs and experiences that we must share if we are to remain faithful in this turbulent and changing world and press forward in Christ to lay hold of life and salvation.

The first disciples who follow Jesus come to him because of the testimonies of others, and in so doing they show how we can all become part of a great chain of witnesses. Jesus's mother and Mary Magdalene, perhaps his closest female disciples, were "women who knew," and they powerfully testified of who Jesus was by their words and actions. Nicodemus can represent the intellectual, someone who is most comfortable with inquiry and discussion yet can still sincerely honor Christ, even if his or her walk of faith is different from others'. The Samaritan woman at the well illustrates the experience of outsiders—whether they differ in terms of gender, ethnicity, or lifestyle—who nonetheless are invited to follow Christ just as those of more "traditional" backgrounds. Followers of all types can experience challenges to their faith, "hard sayings" which might lead them to leave the course of discipleship, but they can stay within the fold if they will stay firmly planted in Jesus and the words of life he brings. Friends of Jesus—like the family of Lazarus, Martha, and Mary—exemplify how discipleship is individual and real, how the Lord is with us in our trials and griefs and can turn all to joy. We can learn from even the seeming foibles and failings of leading disciples such as Peter and Thomas, who show us that anyone can be impulsive but devoted, fallible but faithful.

While these varied characters confirm that there are many ways to experience discipleship and that we should strive to understand fellow believers who have different walks of faith, one character provides the key to what is essential and unifying in the Gospel's message. This is the enigmatic, unnamed figure usually referred to as "the Beloved Disciple." Though usually associated with the apostle John himself, his anonymous appearance in the final chapters of the Gospel allows him to serve as the everyman or everywoman. Leaning on the bosom of the Savior at the

Last Supper, standing at the foot of the cross, and running to the empty tomb, he teaches us what we must believe and become to truly be counted a beloved disciple of our Lord Jesus Christ.

INTRODUCTION

DISCIPLESHIP IN JOHN

Embarking on a Journey through the Fourth Gospel

"But these are written, that ye might believe that Jesus is the Christ, the Son of God; and that believing ye might have life through his name." (John 20:31)

Some years ago when Elder Bruce D. Porter, a member of the First Quorum of the Seventy from 2003 to 2016, was traveling with the Mormon Tabernacle Choir on our tour of the Northeastern United States, he taught me a helpful rubric for better understanding the Atonement of Jesus Christ: the Gospels in the New Testament teach us the facts of the Atonement, the Book of Mormon the doctrine, and the Holy Spirit the application. While I enjoy studying all the scriptures, ever since my mother used to "tell me the stories of Jesus" when I was a child, I have loved to read about the Savior's mortal ministry, his teachings, his saving suffering and death, and his triumphant resurrection in the Bible. I always feel the Spirit when I turn the pages of the Gospels, love teaching the "good news" from these precious texts, and find that by studying and applying them I am better able to come to Christ and learn how to receive his grace (see Moroni 10:32–33).

Because of this, it is not surprising that my favorite class to teach at Brigham Young University is the introductory survey of the New Testament Gospels. Often at the beginning of a new semester, I give my students an informal poll, asking them which of the four Gospels is their favorite. Just a few pick Mark, voting for it, perhaps, because it is the shortest. This is too bad, actually, because this fast-moving and descriptive Gospel, which most scholars believe was the first to be written, provides a powerful and artful testimony that we would do well to understand better. Some pick Matthew, citing such things as its Sermon on the Mount or its masterful portrayal of Jesus as the promised Messiah. More vote for Luke, appreciating not only its beloved Christmas story but also its loving portrayal of the Savior and its focus on women, the poor, and the oppressed. Usually, however, perhaps because of its appealing depiction of Jesus and its moving narrative, the largest number of my students say that their favorite is John, the fourth of the New Testament Gospels.

This is an unfair question, of course, because the Gospel accounts present unique portraits of Jesus that provide different, important insights to his teachings and saving work.[1] They all teach saving truths and have the potential to build testimony. Perhaps it would be better to say that our favorite Gospel is whichever we are studying at that moment. Still, I myself have loved the Gospel of John since I first read it, which sometimes leads me to joke, "We do not have a favorite Gospel, but if we did . . . it would be John!" Without taking away from the value and beauty of the other Gospels, or any other book of scripture, I would like to embark with you on a journey through the Gospel of John, which, I have found, has a powerful potential for bringing us to Christ and deepening our discipleship.

THE APPEAL OF THE GOSPEL OF JOHN

There are a number of reasons why many people are attracted to the Gospel of John. First, it provides unique material not found in Mark, Matthew, and Luke, which are called the synoptic Gospels because they usually tell the story of Jesus from the same point of view. While they present the same basic sequence of events, John is different and preserves unique episodes and powerful teachings. Some of these include several additional visits to Jerusalem, sermons such as the "Discourse on the Bread of Life," and the gripping story of the raising of Lazarus that are not found in the synoptic Gospels. John is also an engaging story, painting moving dialogues and scenes, such as Jesus's discussions with Nicodemus or the Samaritan woman at the well and the poignant portrayal of the mother of Jesus and the Beloved Disciple at the foot of the cross. These draw us as readers into the story, which we feel we are experiencing along with its characters.

John is also very symbolic, and its prologue (John 1:1–51) begins with a hymn that describes Jesus as the premortal and divine Word of God, who is the source of light and life (John 1:1–18; see Appendix A). Later in the Gospel he is portrayed as the well of water springing up into everlasting life (John 4:14); the bread of life (John 6:26–59); the light of the world (John 9:4–5); the good shepherd (John 10:7–16); the way, truth, and the life (John 14:6); and the true vine (John 15:1–10). Even Jesus's miracles are more symbolic in John than they are in the other Gospels, serving more as signs of who he is and what he came to do than they are evidences of his power.[2] John also presents strong, symbolic contrasts, such as light and darkness, life and death, divinity and mortality, and those who reject Jesus and those who accept him, to whom he gives power to become the children of God.[3] John is also the most theological of the Gospels, with its author frequently reflecting upon something that Jesus has said or done, making clear his divinity and how it impacts us as disciples.[4]

These very points, however, have led some secular biblical scholars to question certain features of the Gospel of John. Largely agreed to be the last Gospel written, John presents a much more developed Christology—or understanding of the person and work of Jesus—than the synoptic Gospels, which some commentators have felt reflects the developing understanding that early Christians had of Jesus more than it does knowledge of his first disciples. The evangelists who wrote the four Gospels, however, present different portraits of Jesus and emphasize different features of his nature. Indeed, John's presentation of Jesus as a majestic and divine figure is what has always drawn me to the Gospel of John.[5] Whereas Mark starts with Jesus being declared God's Son by the Father at baptism (Mark 1:10–11) and Matthew and Luke testify of Jesus's divine conception and miraculous birth in their infancy narratives (Matthew 1–2 and Luke 1–2), John begins with Jesus as the Divine Word, which was present with God from the beginning and served as his agent of creation (John 1:1–3).[6]

In fact, to me the Jesus in John is the most like the Christ of the Book of Mormon, whom King Benjamin described as the creator and Lord God Omnipotent who came to the earth to dwell in a tabernacle of clay (Mosiah 3:5); who proclaimed himself "the God of Israel, and the God of the whole earth" to the gathered Nephites in Bountiful (3 Nephi 11:14); and whom the title page describes as the "Eternal God, manifesting himself unto all nations." In short, the Jesus of John is the Christ whom I have come to know, love, and worship. Yet it is not only the powerful testimony of Jesus's divinity in John that helps me come unto Christ. Its focus on discipleship helps me understand what I must believe, know, do, and be in order to better walk with Jesus in my own life. In addition, John's portrayal of characters and their own journey of discipleship helps me relate the story to today's life situations, challenges, and needs.

John's Focus on Discipleship

Discipleship is an important theme of the Gospel of John, highlighted more in this Gospel than in the others. First, the word "disciple" occurs seventy-eight times in John, seventy-one of those times specifically for followers of Jesus. This is much more often than the term appears in the other Gospels or the Book of Acts, which was written by the same author as Luke.[7] Second, John uses the term more broadly than in the other Gospels. In Matthew and Mark, for instance, the term "disciple" is often associated with the twelve special witnesses whom Jesus called as apostles. While Luke sometimes uses the term more broadly, applying it on occasion to the larger groups of people who believe in and follow Jesus as well as to the Twelve, most often John uses the term for people *other* than the Twelve. In fact, John only refers to the Twelve explicitly three times (John 6:67, 70; 20:24), and then three more by implication (13:18; 15:16, 19). He never provides a full list of the Twelve as do Acts and the other Gospels, however, and the word "apostle" does not occur in the English translation of this Gospel at all.[8] The result is that rather than being limited to a smaller group of chosen special witnesses, discipleship appears more broadly as something with which we can match our own experience of trying to follow Jesus.

Anciently, the word "disciple" (Greek, *mathētēs*) suggested not only a student or pupil who learned from a teacher but also an apprentice who strove to become like a master.[9] In other words, being a disciple was not only about *knowing,* it was also about *doing* and *being.* Both Greek philosophers and Jewish teachers (and later rabbis) gathered disciples around them. Like them, Jesus attracted a circle of disciples to himself. This is the portrait of disciples that all of the Gospels paint: Jesus's followers were those who accepted him and his teachings and then followed him. Many of these then literally followed him from place to place to listen to his words and watch his actions, with the result that "follow" (Greek, *akoloutheō*) became a technical word suggesting discipleship.[10] Some, especially in the Twelve but also some of the women close to Jesus, gave up their homes, livelihoods, and even relationships to literally follow him (see Mark 1:18; parallels Matthew 4:18; Luke 5:1, 8:1–3).[11] Others followed him in the sense that they accepted him as their master and strove to live his teachings wherever they lived. Regardless of whether they literally followed him or simply followed him in the way they lived at home, disciples had a sense of mission that led them to bring others to Jesus. Above all, with its greater emphasis on individual discipleship, the Gospel of John portrays a more personal, intimate relationship with the Lord described by strong verbs that define the responsibilities and characteristics of these disciples. The qualities represented by these verbs can help us, as modern-day followers of Christ, understand what we, too, must believe, do, and become.[12]

Words for *believing* and *knowing* appear more often in this gospel than in the others and serve as central features of discipleship. The Greek word for "believe" (*pisteuō*) appears seventy-eight times in John. Beyond simply giving mental assent, however, *pisteuō* additionally connotes trusting and having faith and confidence in someone or something.[13] The importance of placing trust in Christ as the Word is introduced in the prologue, which teaches that those who believe on his name can become the children of God (John 1:12; compare Mosiah 5:17). Closely connected to such belief, confidence, or faith is the importance of knowing. Our King James Version translates two different words as "know," and together they appear 142 times in John. One, the Greek word *ginōskō*, conveys more the sense of acquiring knowledge over time and through experience, as when Jesus taught, "If ye continue in my word, then are ye my disciples indeed; And ye shall *know* the truth, and the truth shall make you free" (John

8:31–32, emphasis added).[14] The other, *oida*, actually comes from the same root as the verb "to see" and indicates a more certain knowledge that comes from seeing, experiencing, or witnessing for oneself.

When it comes to how disciples should *act*, the verbs that are most prominent in John are related to loving, "keeping," and abiding. John uses forms of two verbs for "love" (Greek, *agapaō* and to a lesser extent *phileō*), and these appear more frequently than in the synoptic Gospels.[15] The first reference to love in John occurs in the powerful declaration "For God so *loved* [Greek, *ēgapēsen*] the world, that he gave his only begotten Son" (John 3:16, emphasis added), and from that point on God's love for Jesus, Jesus's love for his disciples, and his disciples' love for him are emphatic themes in the Gospel. Disciples not only love Jesus, they also love and serve one another (John 13:34–35; 15:12–13, 17).[16] Finally, true disciples not only accept Jesus's word, they continue in it and keep his commandments (John 14:15, 23–24; 15:10, 20). In the New Testament, "keep" (Greek, *tēreō*) means more than just observing or obeying. It includes the additional sense of guarding, watching over, and paying attention to. Jesus in John does not give long lists of what disciples should and should not do. Rather, motivated by love and with the direction of the Holy Ghost (see John 14:26), disciples keep Jesus's commandments by seeking his will and eagerly looking for opportunities to bring others to Christ.

I would suggest that Jesus's direction that disciples should abide in him bridges the gap between what we should *do* and what we should *be*. "To abide" (Greek, *menō*), in the sense of dwelling or staying with someone, indicates an ongoing relationship, but it can also suggest persisting or remaining in a way of life or state of being.[17] In John, abiding in the Lord means to continue to love him and others while keeping his commandments, which helps us become more like him. Further, in his discourse on how he is the true vine (John 15:1–17), Jesus describes an organic connection between himself and us. We draw strength and our very spiritual life from him as branches do from the vine. This strength feeds our love for him and enables us to love each other even to the point of sacrificing our very lives, for "Greater love hath no man than this, that a man lay down his life for his friends" (John 15:13). Because the word for "friend" in Greek (*philos*), as in many languages, actually has the same root as "love," employing the language of friendship in John 15:14–15, reveals a new, more intimate relationship between Jesus and his disciples, for we are no longer simply master and servants but beloved friends.

Characters in John

Like other scripture, the Gospel of John is inspired not only in *what* it says but *how* it says it. In other words, it is literature as well as inspired writing. In dramatic literature, characters advance the plot and help readers understand the story and the principles it is trying to teach.[18] Characters in ancient literature, including scripture, were likely to be types as well as representations of historical figures.[19] Because they represent different types of people and their experiences, we can more easily see ourselves in the characters and then apply the scriptures to our own lives.[20] John then illustrates the principles of discipleship through sharply drawn characters who all experience the journey of belief, action, and becoming differently. These include not only individual members of the Twelve, such as Andrew, Peter, Philip, and Thomas, but also an assortment of other well-described, non-apostolic characters—including Nathanael, Nicodemus, the Samaritan woman at the well, Mary of Bethany, her sister Martha, and their brother Lazarus.[21] By not focusing only on special witnesses of Jesus, John succeeds in providing us with a variety of accessible models for discipleship.

The variety of characters and the different trajectories of their walks with Jesus make them valuable models for readers today. As with modern-day disciples, most of the characters in John are presented as encountering Jesus and then needing to make a faith-decision on whether and how to follow him.[22] Andrew, for instance, was already an earnest believer who readily followed Jesus when he received the witness of another. Nicodemus, well-to-do and well-educated, first struggled to understand and accept Jesus but seems to have accepted him in his death. The Samaritan woman was an outsider with a questionable past who was nonetheless open to the truth. Peter and Thomas were devoted but impulsive disciples: at times each slipped or questioned, but both went on to have great faith. Martha and Mary were devoted friends of the Lord whose faith was tested at a time of great loss.

Interestingly some of the best examples of believing in and following Jesus are anonymous in John. Although the mother of Jesus witnessed the first miracle and her son's terrible death, John never names her, even though the original audience and today's readers both knew that she was named Mary. The Samaritan woman, whose beautifully told story teaches us so much about faith and salvation, is also left unnamed, as are the man at the Pool of Bethesda and the man born blind, each of whom Jesus healed. The blind man, in fact, turns out to be an ideal model of discipleship: having received a great gift from the Lord in receiving his sight, he progressively comes to understand who Jesus is and have faith in him, and he testifies of him with increasing boldness in the face of great opposition (John 9:1–34).[23] Such anonymity actually allows us as readers to identify with the characters better. If he or she were named, we might be led to think that only *that* particular person could have that kind of experience, but an unnamed character more easily serves as an everyman or everywoman figure, allowing us to see ourselves in that situation.[24]

The Figure of the Beloved Disciple

The most important unnamed character in the Gospel of John is the figure usually referred to as "the Beloved Disciple." He appears in the second half of the Gospel as "the disciple whom Jesus loved" (John 13:23; 19:26; 20:2; 21:7, 20), and he may be the same as the "other disciple," who along with Peter followed Jesus to the high priest's palace after the Savior's arrest (John 18:15–16). This identification makes it likely that he was also the unnamed disciple of John the Baptist in John 1:35–40, who, along with Andrew, first heard John's testimony and began following Jesus. As the figure who was the "the disciple which testifieth of these things, and wrote these things" (John 21:24), the Beloved Disciple seems to have been an eyewitness of much that Jesus said and did throughout the Gospel, even when he is not explicitly mentioned.[25]

Traditionally, this figure has been identified with John the son of Zebedee, a leading member of the Twelve.[26] If he was the Beloved Disciple, he was either the author, or at least the authoritative source, for the Gospel that bears his name. Issues of authorship and composition are still much discussed in biblical scholarship,[27] and interested readers can consult my treatment of these issues published elsewhere.[28] However, the significance of this anonymous witness for our journey through the Gospel of John is found more in his role as a model disciple.[29] This figure never wavers in his devotion and was a witness of some of the most pivotal moments in the narrative: he leans on Jesus's bosom at the Last Supper, stands at the foot of the cross, and runs to find the empty tomb (John 13:23; 19:26; 20:1–8). While the other characters represent the variety of experiences and testimonies of early disciples—and perhaps today's church members—these three culminating episodes represent the most essential components of a testimony of Jesus Christ and his saving work. Despite our different backgrounds, levels of understanding, and temperaments, we can find common ground and achieve unity as a body of Christ as we focus on these essentials.

LEARNING FROM THE GOSPEL OF JOHN

There are many different ways to study scripture. Sometimes we read the scriptures sequentially, perhaps for a given amount of time each day, while other times we study them topically, moving from passage to passage. Sometimes we may opt for devotional reading, proceeding through passages slowly and prayerfully, pausing to reread and reflect as the Spirit directs us.[30] Other times our study may be more active. As Elder David A. Bednar, a member of the Quorum of the Twelve since 2004, has taught, scripture study is powerful when we search and ask questions as we read, learning vital gospel principles while making connections, discerning patterns, and discovering themes.[31] More academic studies of a text may examine it at two or three levels. The first level is a window into the world of the figures and events that the text represents, and a second level might be another window into the community that preserved this information or for whom it was first written. The third level can be a mirror as we read and interact with the text, one that reflects our understanding of it and the connections that we make with it.[32]

Neither a commentary nor an in-depth scholarly study of the Gospel of John, this book is primarily a devotional reading intended to help us come closer to Christ by learning from the characters who encountered him and responded positively to his call. Still, setting John, and all scripture, in its historical and cultural context helps produce better readings, keeping us from misunderstanding or misinterpreting the text. In other words, trying to understand what the text meant to "them, there, then" helps us more carefully apply it to "us, here, now."[33] Thus, to make John a better mirror, we will still need to see it as a window, better understanding its characters, both historically and as presented in the text. As we do so, we may find that they are more like us than we expected.

As New Testament scholar Brendan Byrne has noted, the purpose of the Gospel of John was to help later readers understand that "they can have an encounter with Jesus every bit as valid and indeed more fruitful" than did many of the original characters.[34] With that in mind, I invite you to join me on a journey of faith, walking through some of the pages of John with prophets and disciples, mothers and sisters, insiders and outsiders, friends and strangers as we all seek to become beloved disciples of our Lord Jesus Christ.

Notes

I am grateful to my longtime assistants, Stephen Betts and Julia Min-tsu Chiou, whose help in the research and editing of this volume was invaluable.

1. Roger R. Keller, "Mark and Luke: Two Facets of a Diamond," in *Sperry Symposium Classics: The New Testament* (ed. Frank F. Judd Jr. and Gaye Strathearn; Provo, UT: Religious Studies Center, Brigham Young University; Salt Lake City: Deseret Book, 2006), 92–107; Richard Holzapfel, *A Lively Hope* (Salt Lake City: Bookcraft, 1999), 1–8.
2. Huntsman, *Miracles of Jesus*, 135–36.
3. See, for instance, the detailed treatment by Craig R. Koester, *Symbolism in the Fourth Gospel* (Minneapolis: Fortress Press, 2003), 141–206, 301–16.
4. See Eric D. Huntsman, "'And the Word Was Made Flesh': A Latter-day Saint Exegesis of the Blood and Water Imagery in the Gospel of John," *Studies in the Bible and Antiquity* 1 (2009): 52–55, 63–65.
5. Throughout his ministry, Jesus's divinity is only thinly veiled: he is in fact the divine Jehovah made flesh (John 1:14), who knows all things (John 13:3; 18:4; 19:28), does what he has seen the Father do (John 5:17–20), reveals the Father (John 1:18; 14:7–10), and has power to lay down his life and take it up again (John 10:18; 15:13).

6. See Eric D. Huntsman, "The Lamb of God: Unique Aspects of the Passion Narrative in John," in *Behold the Lamb of God: The Fourth Annual BYU Religious Education Easter Conference* (eds. Richard Neitzel Holzapfel, Frank F. Judd, Jr., and Thomas A. Wayment; Provo, Utah: Religious Studies Center, 2008), 49–52.
7. See Raymond F. Collins, "'Who Are You?' Comparison/Contrast and Fourth Gospel Characterization," *Characters and Characterization in the Gospel of John*, ed. Christopher W. Skinner, Library of New Testament Studies 461 (New York: Bloomsbury, 2013), 85. Compare this with 46 times in Mark, 72 times in Matthew, 37 times in Luke, and 28 times in Acts. See P. Nepper-Christensen, "mathētēs," *Exegetical Dictionary of the New Testament*, edited by Horst Balz and Gerhard Schneider, 3 vols. (Grand Rapids: Eerdmans, 1990), 2.372.
8. While the Greek word *apostolos* does appear in John 13:16, it is used there in such a non-technical sense that the KJV simply renders it "he that is sent."
9. Walter Bauer, "mathētēs," *A Greek-English Lexicon of the New Testament and Other Early Christian Literature*, edited by Frederick William Danker, translated by William F. Arndt, F. Wilbur Gingrich, and F.W. Danker, 3rd edition (Chicago: University of Chicago, 2000), 609–10.
10. P. Nepper-Christensen, "mathētēs,", 2.372–74. See also Bauer, "akoloutheō," *Greek-English Lexicon*, 36–37.
11. Michael J. Wilkins, "Disciples," Dictionary of Jesus and the Gospels (Dower's Grove, Ill.: InterVarsity Press, 1992), 177, *Patterns of Discipleship in the New Testament*, ed. by Richard N. Longenecker (Grand Rapids: Eerdmans, 1996), 1–5.
12. See Melvyn R. Hillmer, "They Believed in Him: Discipleship in the Johannine Tradition," *Patterns of Discipleship in the New Testament*, 84–93.
13. Bauer, "pisteuō," *Greek-English Lexicon*, 816–18; G. Barth, "pisteuō," *Exegetical Dictionary of the New Testament*, 3.92–93, 95–96.
14. Bauer, "ginōskō" and "oida," *Greek-English Lexicon*, 199–201, 693–94; W. Schmithals, "ginōskō," and A. Horstmann, "oida," *Exegetical Dictionary of the New Testament*, 1.57, 250–51; 2.493–94.
15. G. Schneider, "agapaō" and W. Feneberg, "*phileō*," *Exegetical Dictionary of the New Testament*, 1.8, 11–12; 3.425–26.
16. R. Alan Culpepper, *Anatomy of the Fourth Gospel* (Philadelphia: Fortress Press, 1983), 115–19.
17. Bauer, "menō," *Greek-English Lexicon*, 630–31.
18. Nancy Roser, Miriam Martinez, Charles Fuhrken, and Kathleen McDonnold, "Characters as Guides to Meaning," *The Reading Teacher* 60.6 (2007): 548–559.

19. Our word "character" comes from the Greek *charaktēr*, which originally derived from a word referring to the mark, impression, or stamp made by a seal or brand (Bauer, "charagma" and "charaktēr" *Greek-English Lexicon*, 1077–78). Because ancient literature focused more on action than on the actors, according to Aristotle characters tended to represent the kinds of things that different people would do (*Poetics* 1450a15–23).
20. Colleen M. Conway, *Men and Women in the Fourth Gospel: Gender and Johannine Characterization* (Atlanta: Society of Biblical Literature, 1999), 42–45; Christopher W. Skinner, *Characters and Characterization in the Gospel of John*, (Bloomsbury, Ill.: Bloomsbury T&T Clark, 2013), xvii–xxxii.
21. Richard Bauckham, *Jesus and the Eyewitnesses* (Grand Rapids: Eerdmans, 2006), 402.
22. Cornelis Bennema, *Encountering Jesus: Character Studies in the Gospel of John* (Minneapolis: Fortress Press, 2014), x, 30, 36–37, 366–71; Christopher Skinner, *Reading John*, (Eugene, Oreg.: Cascade Books, 2015), 103.
23. Raymond Collins, "From John to the Beloved Disciple: An Essay on Johannine Characters," *Interpretation* 49 (1995): 364–65; Skinner, *Reading John*, 107.
24. David Beck, "The Narrative Function of Anonymity in the Fourth Gospel," *Semeia* 63 (1993): 146–53. For a somewhat different explanation of this anonymity, see Richard Bauckham, *The Testimony of the Beloved Disciple* (Grand Rapids: Baker Academic), 90–91.
25. Raymond E. Brown, *The Gospel according to John*, Anchor Bible 29–29A (New York: Doubleday, 1966), xcii–xcviii; Richard Bauckham, *Jesus and the Eyewitnesses,* 390–93, 402–403; Bennema, *Encountering Jesus*, 299–30; Marianne Meye Thompson, *John* (Louisville, Kent.: Westminster John Knox Press, 2015), 17–19.
26. Other possibilities include Lazarus, who is explicitly described in John 11:5 as being someone whom Jesus loved, as well as an otherwise unknown early Christian leader called "John the elder." See Brown, *Gospel according to John*, lxxxviii–xcii; Morris, *Gospel according to John*, 4–25; Conway, *Men and Women in the Fourth Gospel*, 177–78; Bennema, *Encountering Jesus*, 309–313.
27. Brown, *Gospel according to John*, xcviii–cii; Leon Morris, *The Gospel according to John*, The New International Commentary on the New Testament (Grand Rapids: Eerdmans, 1995), 4–25; Bauckham, *Jesus and the Eyewitnesses*, 393–402, and *Testimony of the Beloved Disciple*, 73–90.
28. Richard Neitzel Holzapfel, Eric D, Huntsman, and Thomas A. Wayment, *Jesus Christ and the World of the New Testament* (Salt Lake City: Deseret Book: 2006), 126–130; Eric D. Huntsman, "The Gospel according to

John," in *New Testament History, Culture, and Society*, edited by Lincoln Blumell (Springville, Utah: Cedar Fort, 2018 forthcoming).

29. Beck, "The Narrative Function of Anonymity in the Fourth Gospel," *Semeia* 63 (1993): 153–55, and "'Whom Jesus Loved': Anonymity and Identity, Belief and Witness in the Fourth Gospel," *Characters and Characterization in the Gospel of John*, 221–23.
30. Eric D. Huntsman, *Worship: Adding Depth to Your Devotion* (Salt Lake City: Deseret Book, 2016), 108–110.
31. David A. Bednar, "A Reservoir of Living Water," *Brigham Young University 2006–2007 Speeches* (Provo: Brigham Young University Publications and Graphics, 2006–2007), 1–10.
32. Culpepper, *Anatomy of the Fourth Gospel*, 1–5; Conway, *Men and Women in the Fourth Gospel*, 40–41.
33. Eric D. Huntsman, "Teaching through Exegesis: Helping Students Ask Questions of the Text," *Religious Educator* 6.1 (Winter 2005), 107–126.
34. Brendan Byrne, "The Faith of the Beloved Disciple and the Community in John 20," *Journal for the Study of the New Testament* 23 (1985): 93.

Chapter 1

The First Disciples

Come and See

"The next day John seeth Jesus coming unto him, and saith, Behold the Lamb of God, which taketh away the sin of the world . . . And the two disciples heard him speak, and they followed Jesus." (John 1:29, 37)

Whereas the disciples' understanding of who Jesus is and what he has come to do unfolds slowly throughout the narratives of the synoptic Gospels, characters in John come to believe and accept who Jesus is from the beginning of the narrative, seeing him as the true Light (John 1:7–8), the Lamb of God (1:29, 39), the Messiah or Christ (1:41), and the Son of God and King of Israel (1:49). The first character in this Gospel, after Jesus as the premortal Divine Word, is the prophet John, known in the other Gospels as John the Baptist. His witness of Jesus was accepted by two of his own followers, Andrew and another unnamed disciple. Andrew, in turn, shared his testimony with his brother Peter, and Jesus was then introduced to their friend Philip. When Philip received their testimonies, he next found another friend, Nathanael.

While the first testimony in this chain of witnesses, that of the prophet John, came directly by revelation, those of subsequent disciples began simply by their accepting in faith what they heard. As the Lord revealed to Joseph Smith, "To some it is given by the Holy Ghost to know that Jesus Christ is the Son of God, and that he was crucified for the sins of the world. To others it is given to believe on their words, that they also might have eternal life if they continue faithful" (D&C 46:13–14). This chain reflects a pattern that continues today: when we hear the good news of the salvation that comes through Jesus Christ, we share it with students, family, and friends, eagerly inviting them to "Come and see" (see John 1:39).

These characters in John do more than provide us a window into the faith of the first disciples. They also provide us a mirror in which we can view our own walk with the Lord, seeing how the seeds of our testimony were planted and how we can share that witness with others. The titles that these first disciples give Jesus reflect what we as disciples should *believe* about him, and their choice to follow him and share their faith show us we should *do*. At this point in the story, however, their discipleship is still new. As is often the case with us, at the outset of their journey of faith it is not yet clear what they will *become*, but they have started on the path with him who was "the way, the truth, and the life" (see John 14:6).

THE PROPHET JOHN

Unlike the synoptic Gospels, which present John as a preacher of repentance and a baptizer, the evangelist who wrote the Fourth Gospel primarily casts him as a witness. In fact, the Fourth Gospel neither uses the title "the Baptist" nor does it actually depict John as baptizing Jesus.[1] Instead, he is introduced in the prologue itself, where two descriptions of John in straightforward prose interrupt the poetic, hymnic description of the Divine Word.[2] The first stresses that he was not the Light but rather was sent as a witness of the Light whose testimony was meant to help others believe (John 1:6–8). The second records one of his main messages, that "He that cometh after me is preferred before me: for he was before me" (John 1:15), testifying at once to Jesus's higher status and to his premortal existence. As a witness, then, John is portrayed primarily as a prophet, and it is in this role that he encounters representatives of the Jerusalem authorities, who have come to find out who he is. Testifying that he is not the Christ, nor Elijah (KJV, "Elias"), nor the prophet promised by Moses, he maintains that he was fulfilling the role foreseen by Isaiah in preparing the way of the Lord. Instead he testifies of his own relative unworthiness to the one for whom he is preparing the way (John 1:19–28).

The next day when John saw Jesus walking by, he proclaimed, "Behold the Lamb of God, which taketh away the sin of the world" (John 1:29). With this testimony, the prophet John established one of the most important images of the Gospel of John, one that is fulfilled with the Crucifixion, when Jesus, as the spotless Passover lamb, died that we might live.[3] At some point between this proclamation and his earlier interchange with the representatives of the Jewish authorities, John appears to have baptized Jesus, because he now testifies that he had while baptizing seen the Spirit descending upon Jesus as a dove. This was a sign that not only would Jesus baptize with the Holy Ghost, but that he was indeed the Son of God (John 1:29–34).

John rejoiced in his role, which was subordinate to the one for whom he was a witness. He later describes himself to his own followers as a best man who was glad just to hear the voice of the bridegroom and declared, "He must increase, but I must decrease" (John 3:29–30).[4] This relationship reflects the experience of prophets in every age who love the word of the Lord and rejoice to share it with us. Indeed, the Gospel of John's focus on John the Baptist as a prophetic witness of Jesus Christ—almost to the exclusion of other important parts of his ministry—provides us with an important mirror in understanding our own experience with prophets in our dispensation. As authorized servants and spokesmen for the Lord, modern-day prophets teach and do many important, and vital, things. I am struck, however, with the fact that their primary role is always as a witness of God our Father and the divine identity and mission of his Son, Jesus Christ. For example, the prophet of the Restoration, Joseph Smith, brought forth the Book of Mormon, received the priesthood, reorganized the Church of Jesus Christ, gathered the saints, and initiated temple work in this dispensation, but Joseph's First Vision in the Sacred Grove and the striking vision of the Father and the Son in D&C 76:11–24 stand out to me as being among the Prophet's most important accomplishments.

Andrew and the Other Disciple

John the prophet passed on this powerful witness to two of his own followers, Andrew and another disciple who remains nameless, when he pointed Jesus out to them and repeated the declaration that he was the Lamb of God (John 1:35–36). Presumably, these two disciples had been present during John's earlier declaration and understood what this meant, that Jesus was the Son of God chosen to bear the sin of the world. Sin appears to be used here comprehensively as it is in the early letters of Paul to represent not just an individual transgression but also the fallen state that the world—both the society of people on it and perhaps even the physical world—finds itself in. How well John's two disciples understood the theological implications of this first is unclear, but they immediately followed (Greek, *ēkolouthēsan*, from *akoloutheō*) Jesus (John 1:37), using the word that was also employed to signal that one was attaching him or herself to a new master as a disciple.

Their act of following Jesus signaled that they believed the testimony of John, having enough trust or confidence in it to change their allegiance and literally change where they lived. When Jesus saw them following him and asked what they wanted, they immediately asked where he was staying (Greek, *meneis*; KJV, "where dwellest thou?"). This is the same word that the Gospel of John later uses for "abide" in Jesus's "Farewell Discourses" (see John 15:1–11), perhaps suggesting that they were not only prepared to change their living accommodations but were also pledging to persist in the new path of discipleship that they had chosen. Jesus's famous response, "Come and see," was then an invitation for them to spend time with him, learn his doctrine, and see whether it was, in fact, of God (see John 7:17).

Andrew at this point is still a rather "flat," or undeveloped, character; without giving any background or further descriptions, John uses him primarily as a type whose role here focuses more on his actions than his historical identity.[5] This is even more the case with the other disciple, who remains anonymous and can then stand for any one of us as we read the story. Andrew is relatively undeveloped compared to other characters in John, but he still receives considerably more attention in this Gospel than he does in the others. In the synoptic Gospels he simply appears in his role as Peter's brother, but in John he is an independent actor and functions later as an active disciple and witness to others. This growth is even more apparent if the other, unnamed follower is, in fact, the same as the figure of the Beloved Disciple.[6] Here he simply receives the witness of the prophet John and acts upon it by following Jesus. By the end of the Gospel, however, he will have become the ideal disciple, one who has received the most important witnesses of the identity and role of Jesus Christ.

The growth of these two followers of John is the result of their choice to "Come and see." Their act of accepting an invitation to know the Savior better represents how we can respond to what we hear from prophets like John—especially the fact that Jesus is both the Lamb and Son of God, come to take away all our sin. If we are not careful, however, this core belief can get lost in our perceived need to understand and accept the entirety of the history, teachings, and experience of the Church and its people in the almost two centuries that have passed since its restoration. In an address called "Come and See," Elder Jeffrey R. Holland wisely counseled us, "My desire for you is to have more straightforward experience with the Savior's life and teachings. Perhaps sometimes we come to Christ too obliquely, focusing on structure or methods or elements of Church administration. Those are important, but not without attention to the weightier matters of the kingdom, first and foremost of which is a personal spiritual relationship with Deity, including the Savior whose kingdom this is."[7]

Perhaps overlooked in this brief call story is the difficulty that Andrew and his friend may have felt leaving their old master, even for one as perfect as their new Master. However, there is a powerful lesson in their exchange of the prophet John for the Lord Jesus. We naturally become attached to our own witnesses, from parents and teachers all the way to prophets, making it difficult to "switch loyalties," when change comes. I know in my own case the transitions after the deaths of long-serving Church presidents, such as those of President Spencer W. Kimball or President Gordon B. Hinckley, were difficult. Having been blessed by their examples, teaching, and witness, I mourned their passing and wondered how I could appreciate their successors nearly as much. However, without fail, when a new president speaks with the authority of his calling and bears powerful testimony of the Lord Jesus Christ, I realize that as much as we love and appreciate individual leaders, our discipleship is to the Lord himself.

PETER AND PHILIP

Andrew's brother Simon and his friend Philip are the next two disciples presented as characters in John's Gospel, but unlike Andrew and the other disciple, who appear and act together, they receive the news of Jesus separately and respond to it differently. Andrew "first findeth his own brother Simon, and saith unto him, We have found the Messias, which is, being interpreted, the Christ" (John 1:41). Having obtained his own testimony of Jesus, Andrew naturally wanted to share it with someone in his family, and he personally brought Simon to Jesus, who gave him the new name of Cephas or "Rock" (Aramaic, *Kēphâ*; Greek, *Petros*) by which he is better known (John 1:41–42).[8] Simon Peter is the most frequently mentioned and in many ways best-developed character in John after Jesus himself,[9] which makes his depiction in this first scene so interesting. With a reputation for being strong, active, and even impetuous, in his introduction he is largely passive: Andrew finds him and brings him to Jesus, who renames Simon without the latter ever saying or doing a thing. He is, in fact, the only one in this succession of new disciples who does not attribute a Christological title to Jesus or actively share his witness with someone else.[10]

Since names were seen as reflecting character in the ancient world, the renaming of Simon was a significant act but one that here seems to have suggested potentiality more than his current state. The name *Peter* later came to indicate this leading disciple's steadfastness and strength, but he would go through much to realize these qualities. Here he starts simply as the recipient of the witness that Jesus was the Messiah, and he goes through many ups and downs in the course of the narrative before he receives his final approbation and commission in the epilogue of the Gospel (John 21). Some, in fact, have seen his characterization as a rock as being somewhat ironic given the vicissitudes of his career before the resurrection of Jesus.[11] I prefer to see it as a metaphor that Simon Peter is at this point a piece of stone who will be carved and polished through the course of his discipleship. Even Joseph Smith's inspired addition that rock here can also refer to "a seer, or a stone" (JST John 1:42) can be seen in this developmental light. He has received the kernel of his eventually certain knowledge that Jesus is the Christ (see 2 Peter 1:16–19) and has been set on the path to his later prophetic role as shepherd, leader of the Church, and martyr (see John 21:15–19; compare Matthew 16:17–19).

The calls of Andrew and Peter in John's Gospel differ from the stories told in the synoptic Gospels, where they are called from their fishing nets together with James and John, the two sons of Zebedee (see Mark 1:16–20; parallels Matthew 4:18–22; Luke 5:1–11). Perhaps a way to harmonize this discrepancy is that John is giving us their initial call to discipleship, but the synoptic Gospels are recording a later call to the full-time ministry following Jesus's forty-day period of preparation in the desert. Regardless, John's unique call stories are significant because they are meant to show us how they were prepared to be disciples.[12]

Next Jesus, or perhaps Andrew himself, found Philip, who responded to the call to follow Jesus (John 1:43).[13] Philip, who like Andrew had a Greek name, was from Bethsaida, the Hellenized city on the Sea of Galilee that was also the hometown of Philip and Andrew. Andrew and Philip appear to have known each other and even to have been friends. In all subsequent appearances of Andrew in John, he always appears paired with Philip, next trying to solve the problem of feeding the five thousand (John 6:5–9) and then working together to introduce some Greeks to Jesus (John 12:20–22). With these two calls, therefore, we see the circle of discipleship expanding to the family and friends of an earlier believer. Indeed, the responsibility of bringing others to Jesus, as we shall see, is a fundamental part of discipleship in the Gospel of John.

NATHANAEL

Accepting the call to follow Jesus, Philip found Nathanael, another prospective disciple, testifying, "We have found him, of whom Moses in the law, and the prophets, did write, Jesus of Nazareth . . ." (John 1:45). Because of the insignificance of Nazareth and perhaps because it was not mentioned in any of the Old Testament prophecies, Nathanael's first reaction, "Can there any good thing come out of Nazareth?" (John 1:46) was perhaps scornful, even sarcastic. Philip was not cowed by his friend's response but simply repeated the invitation, "Come and see." When Jesus sees Nathanael coming to him, he exclaims, "Behold an Israelite indeed, in whom is no guile!" (John 1:47), which can be taken two ways. Often it is seen as an insightful commendation of Nathanael, who, unlike the patriarch Jacob who was renamed Israel, was known for his trickiness (see Genesis 27:6–27; 30:25–43).[14] Conversely, it could have been a wry observation indicating that Jesus knew the disparaging comment that Nathanael had just made about Nazareth.[15]

This would help explain Nathanael's surprise that Jesus already knows him. Jesus then shares something else that Nathanael had been doing, apparently having a private moment under a fig tree (see John 1:48). This leads Nathanael to utter one of the strongest declarations regarding Jesus that anyone has expressed in this series of episodes: "Rabbi, thou art the Son of God; thou art the King of Israel" (John 1:49).[16] While we do not know what Nathanael had been doing under the fig tree, conceivably he had been having a spiritual experience, perhaps praying about the very question of the coming of the Messiah and the deliverance of Israel. If so, Jesus's direct address to his questions reminds me of the revelation that the Lord gave Oliver Cowdery during one of his periods of questioning: "Verily, verily, I say unto you, if you desire a further witness, cast your mind upon the night that you cried unto me in your heart, that you might know concerning the truth of these things. Did I not speak peace to your mind concerning the matter? What greater witness can you have than from God?" (D&C 6:22–23).

Jesus follows Nathanael's strong Christological declaration with a promise of yet greater revelations: "Hereafter ye shall see heaven open, and the angels of God ascending and descending upon the Son of man" (John 1:51). This is an echo of the experience of the patriarch Jacob's vision at Bethel in which he saw a ladder by which angels ascended and descended in and out of heaven that Jesus connects with his own mission to redeem the world and bring them to the Father. Jesus's use of these scriptural allusions and references suggests that Nathanael had strong Jewish expectations. He is, I would suggest, a type of a good, already strongly believing person whose faith finds fulfillment and expansion in his new discipleship. In that regard, he reminds me of the many honorable, religious people whose previous faith and spiritual experiences prepare them for and lead them to the restored Church when disciples of Christ share their witness.

Unlike Andrew, Peter, and Philip, Nathanael does not appear in any of the preserved lists of the Twelve (Mark 3:14–19; Matthew 10:1–4; Luke 6:13–16; Acts 1:13). While he has been traditionally associated with Bartholomew,[17] John presents him as a simple, individual disciple rather than an apostle. In that regard, it is perhaps significant that he has the most detailed interaction with Jesus of any in this succession of witnesses and new disciples. His example, and perhaps that of the unnamed follower of the prophet John, suggests that all of us can have a personal relationship with Jesus, one accompanied by significant revelation. Nathanael is not mentioned again until the epilogue, where he is listed as one of seven disciples who meet the Risen Lord on the shore of the Sea of Galilee (John 21:2). This disciple, who received a personal call and a promise of revelation at the beginning of his walk with the Lord, in the end receives a firm witness and sure knowledge.

Part of a Great Chain of Witnesses

The missionary efforts of Andrew and Philip exemplify the natural pattern for us as modern-day disciples: finding the truth, we are eager to share it with both family and friends, and we then often have the joy of serving together in the kingdom. While I was born and raised in the Church, like most people I have needed to be grounded and strengthened in an ongoing process of conversion. My conversions have been from the Spirit, but the seeds of faith were planted and nurtured by my mother, father, and other loved ones. Like many in the Church, I am grateful that I had the chance to share my testimony of Jesus and his restored gospel on my mission. Now, as a husband and father, I have the great joy of sharing my faith with my family.

As a young man and now as an adult, the influence of faithful, believing friends has continued to be invaluable. Many of my close friends have been ones with whom I have served in the Church—on my mission, in bishoprics, and in the Mormon Tabernacle Choir—because the process of sharing our testimonies of Christ through word, service, and music has brought us together. I love the words taken from the welcome given in the Kirtland School of the Prophets: "Art thou a brother or brethren? I salute you in the name of the Lord Jesus Christ, in token or remembrance of the everlasting covenant, in which covenant I receive you to fellowship, in a determination that is fixed, immovable, and unchangeable, to be your friend and brother through the grace of God in the bonds of love, to walk in all the commandments of God blameless, in thanksgiving, forever and ever. Amen" (D&C 88:133).

The testimonies and discipleship of prophets and parents, family and friends, and leaders and teachers have blessed many of us. Our relationship with the Lord then impels us to share our own witness with those outside our faith, perhaps bringing them into the Church, even as we seek to strengthen friends and families within it. When we do so, like the prophet John, Andrew, Peter, Philip, and Nathanael, we become part of a great, beloved chain of witnesses.

NOTES

1. Bennema, *Encountering Jesus*, 61–63.
2. For the prologue (John 1:1–18) as an early Christian hymn, see Appendix A. It is unclear where the testimony of John that begins in 1:15 ends, but I take 1:16–18 as the first of several reflections by the narrator that interrupt the narrative of the Gospel of John.
3. Huntsman, "The Lamb of God," 52–55, 62.
4. See Bennema, *Encountering Jesus*, 67–69.
5. Conway, *Men and Women in the Fourth Gospel*, 58; Bennema, *Encountering Jesus*, 109.
6. Bennema, *Encountering Jesus*, 300.
7. Jeffrey R. Holland, "Come and See," *The New Era* (December 1997): 4, 6.
8. Bennema, *Encountering Jesus*, 111–12.
9. John 1:40–42; 6:67–69; 13:6–11, 22–23–26, 36–38; 18:10–11, 15–18, 25–27;20:2–10; 21:1–23. See Culpepper, *Anatomy of the Fourth Gospel*, 120–21; Conway, *Men and Women in the Fourth Gospel*, 163–64.
10. Conway, *Men and Women in the Fourth Gospel*, 165–66.
11. Bennema, *Encountering Jesus*, 111–112.
12. Brown, *Gospel according to John*, 77–78.
13. The Greek text relating the call of Philip is actually ambiguous in the original. Our King James Version reads, "The day following <Jesus> *would go forth* into Galilee, and findeth Philip, and saith unto him, Follow me" (John 1:43, emphasis added). Because the text for "would go forth" (Greek, *ēthelēsan exelthein*) lacks an expressed subject, a more literal translation would be "The next day *he* wanted to go to Galilee, and he found Philip." So while Jesus may have been the active finder in this verse, it is also possible that Philip "first findeth his own brother Simon" (v. 41), and then found Philip in their hometown of Bethsaida (vv. 43–44). See Bennema, *Encountering Jesus*, 102.
14. Marianne Meye Thompson, *John: A Commentary*, New Testament Library (Louisville, Kent.: Westminster John Knox Press, 2015), 52.
15. Brown, *Gospel according to John*, 87; Bennema, *Encountering Jesus*, 130 and n. 17.
16. Brown, *Gospel according to John*, 77–78.
17. Brown, *Gospel according to John*, 82 n. 45 Morris, *Gospel according to John*, 143–44; Bennema, *Encountering Jesus*, 128–29.

Chapter 2

The Mother of Jesus and Mary Magdalene

Women as Witnesses

"His mother saith unto the servants, Whatsoever he saith unto you, do it." (John 2:5)

Two of the most prominent female disciples in the Gospel of John appear in the narrative with already-established relationships with the Lord. This contrasts with the first disciples, who began their discipleship by first receiving the witness of others before they began to follow Jesus themselves. The mother of Jesus first appears at the wedding at Cana (John 2:1–11), where she plays a prominent role in effecting the first miraculous sign recorded in John's Gospel. Unlike Matthew or Luke, John does not include an infancy narrative or any story from Jesus's childhood, nor does he ever even name Jesus's mother. As his mother, however, she had known Jesus longer and better than anyone else. She then appears again at the Crucifixion scene, standing at the foot of the cross with the Beloved Disciple and two or three other women (John 19:25–27).[1] One of these is Mary Magdalene, whose presence at Jesus's execution suggests that she was close to him. Luke had recorded that she had been a close disciple who had traveled with Jesus since Galilee (Luke

8:1–3), and John portrays her as one of his most developed characters in a powerfully moving scene at the empty tomb (John 20:1–3, 11–18).

These two women, each close to Jesus, also function as strong witnesses of him, motivating others to believe and then act in faith. The mother of Jesus certainly understood what it meant that he was the Son of God. Not only had she shown confidence in his power to bless others, she was also able to motivate and lead others to act in faith. Both women were eyewitnesses of the Crucifixion, watching the Lamb of God die for the sin of the world, and Mary Magdalene was the first to see, and touch, the Risen Lord. The importance of their testimonies is striking given the time and culture in which they lived, when the witness of a woman was not even admissible in court.[2] Their examples show us the importance of every person's discipleship—regardless of sex, ethnicity, economic status, or other background—and encourage us to learn from and be led by such women of faith today.

The Wedding at Cana

According to John, the mother of Jesus attended a marriage at Cana to which he and his newly called disciples had also been invited (John 2:1–2). She appears in the narrative before they do, however, and she is the one who drives the action. Given her role in the episode and how well known Mary is in the other Gospels, it is curious that John does not name her. Her anonymity here, however, is likely for the same reason that the Beloved Disciple is also left nameless: she, like him, can stand as a type for those followers of Jesus who are closest to him, having loving relationships that are like family. As the only character who clearly appears at the beginning and end of John's narrative (unless the other disciple of John 1:35–40 is the Beloved Disciple), her appearances frame Jesus's public ministry,[3] making her a prime witness of her son.

Cana was a town in lower Galilee not far from Nazareth, the hometown of Jesus according to the synoptic Gospels, and Capernaum, the base for his Galilean ministry. John does not provide any details about the wedding, leaving the bride, the groom, and other guests anonymous as well. While there has been speculation at their identity and the connection of Jesus's family to the wedding party,[4] this perhaps overlooks the symbolism of the wedding feast. Throughout the Old Testament, the covenant relationship between *YHWH*, or Jehovah, and his people is described as a marriage. In the New Testament, Jesus is described as the bridegroom and the Church as the bride.[5] Whereas the relationship between the Lord and his people was never fully realized in the Old Testament, now that Jesus is the Word made flesh, Jehovah has at last come to join his people and actually live with them.[6]

When Jesus's mother learned that the wedding feast had run out of wine, she approached Jesus and informed him (John 2:3). Although she did not specifically ask him to remedy the situation, she appears confident that he would do something to help. His response is enigmatic and has led to a variety of interpretations: "Jesus saith unto her, *Woman*, what have I to do with thee? mine hour is not yet come" (John 2:4, emphasis added). A better way of translating the original "What have I to do with thee?" (Greek, *ti emoi kai soi*) is "What does this have to do with us?"[7] and Joseph Smith's New Translation rendered it, "Woman, what wilt thou have me to do for thee? that will I do; for mine hour is not yet come" (JST John 2:4). Jesus's reference to his hour not yet having come can refer either to his final hour, as it does later in John in reference to his crucifixion (see John 7:30; 8:20; 12:23, 27–28; 13:1; 16:32; 17:1), or simply to mean that his formal, public ministry had not yet begun (see 4:23; 5:23).

His calling his mother "woman" (Greek, *gynai*), however, is more problematic. Although there are examples of Jesus speaking to other women this way,[8] in this context it seems curt, especially considering that there are no examples in Jewish or Greek sources of a son calling his mother "woman" as a form of address.[9] There have been frequent efforts to soften this phrase, noting that his use of the vocative form of *gynē* could simply be a polite title,[10] such as calling her "lady" or something such as "ma'am." However, given that the mother of Jesus is purposefully left anonymous, she may have been called "woman" simply for typological reasons. More broadly, it could connect her with other archetypal women such as Eve, whom Adam called "woman" (Genesis 2:22–23) and who continues to be addressed as such throughout the Creation narrative (Genesis 3:15–16). Similarly, a figurative woman appears in Revelation 12, representing everything from Mary the mother of Jesus to the Church in the last days.[11] Within the Gospel of John itself, it certainly links her with other women who serve as types of how Jesus interacts with his disciples (see John 4:21; 8:10; 20:13, 15).

Despite the ambiguity of Jesus's response, his mother turned to the servants and directed them to do whatever Jesus told them. Jesus unexpectedly asked them to fill six large water pots used for Jewish ritual purification. When they obediently complied, he had the servants draw from them to give a drink to the "governor," or master, of the feast, who found that the water had become fine wine (John 2:5–9). This was the first of the miraculous signs (Greek, *sēmeia*) in John, one that "manifested forth his glory" and caused Jesus's disciples to believe and have confidence in him (2:11).

While there are many ways to interpret the symbolism of this miracle, one powerful way to understand it is as a sign of how Jesus is the Creator. As the Divine Word he created, and now, as the Incarnate Word, he can recreate or reorganize the elements.[12] His mother may or may not have known beforehand that he was able to do this, but her confidence in him brought others to this knowledge. In this, she was like the Prophet John, leading others to Christ.

The Mother of Jesus and the Incarnation

Another way of interpreting the miracle of the water turned to wine underscores the important role of Mary, the mother of Jesus, in his incarnation. The use of water in this miracle connects it to the many other references to water in John's Gospel, where it consistently represents eternal life, spirit, and divinity (John 3:5; 4:10–15; 5:3–4; 7:38). Particularly in a sacramental sense, wine can represent blood. While John's Gospel does not explicitly describe the institution of the sacrament as do the synoptic Gospels, it certainly alludes to it in the Bread of Life discourse when Jesus speaks of symbolically eating his flesh and drinking his blood (John 6:53–57). As part of the standard formulation "bodies of flesh and blood," blood is implicitly tied to mortality.[13] As such, it contrasts with the eternal or divine life represented by water. With these symbols in mind, we can also see the miraculous sign of Jesus's turning water into wine as a symbol of his own incarnation: the Premortal Divine Word became the Man Jesus.[14]

This interpretation makes Mary's presence at Cana all the more significant. Just as she was the catalyst for the miracle, prompting her son to act, so she was a necessary agent in making the Word flesh (compare John 1:14). The miracle at Cana is, in a sense, the Gospel of John's equivalent of an infancy narrative. What Matthew 1–2 and Luke 1–2 do explicitly in their narratives, John does symbolically. In this case, Jesus's disciples believe on him not only because the miraculous sign demonstrated for them that he was the Creator but also because it spoke to his condescension in the flesh. Though currently veiled in mortal flesh, the miracle attests his divinity.

Not only was Jesus's mother a witness that he was the Son of God, she was the very instrument of bringing him into the world. As a type, however, these same roles extend to us. We, too, can be witnesses of Christ's divinity and be catalysts in bringing others to him, helping them become recipients of his grace. According to the well-loved canticle called the *Magnificat*, Mary "magnified the Lord" (Luke 1:46–55) by conceiving and bearing the Babe of Bethlehem. In a similar way, we can seek to magnify the Risen Christ by bringing him into the world through our lives and testimonies every day.

Standing at the Foot of the Cross

In a powerful and poignant scene, the mother of Jesus next appears in the Gospel of John standing at the cross (John 19:25). Unlike the wedding of Cana, where she was an active participant, here she is a passive witness of her son's suffering and death. She shared this experience with a few other women, but the other important figure besides Mary is that of the Beloved Disciple. To them Jesus declared, "'*Woman*, behold thy son!' Then saith he to the disciple, 'Behold thy mother!' And from that hour that disciple took her unto his own home" (John 19:26–27, emphasis added). Jesus again referred to his mother as "woman" (Greek, *gynai*), perhaps generalizing her and connecting her to the other important women in the Gospel and to women—and all disciples—in every age.

Not all commentators agree on what Jesus was doing when he commended his mother and the Beloved Disciple to each other. Some, taking the incident as primarily historical, see this as Jesus making arrangements for his mother's care after his death.[15] Others prefer to see the exchange symbolically, using it to understand the situation of the early Christian community or as a mirror reflecting our own relationships with the Lord.[16] Taking the symbolic approach, perhaps we should focus on the Beloved Disciple as much as we do on Mary. If he effectively became a new son to Mary, then he also entered into a new relationship with Jesus. Now in the position of a brother, the disciple had moved from being a follower to being a member of the family. In other words, the saving death of Jesus restored us to our rightful place as children of God (see John 1:12), "For through him we both have access by one Spirit unto the Father. Now therefore ye are no more strangers and foreigners, but fellow citizens with the saints, and of the household of God" (Ephesians 2:18–19).

After Jesus voluntarily laid down his life, surrendering his spirit with the words "It is finished" (John 19:30), soldiers broke the legs of the two criminals who were crucified beside him. This was meant to hasten their deaths before the setting of the sun, which in John marks not only the onset of the Sabbath but also the beginning of Passover (John 19:31–32).[17] Finding Jesus already dead, however, they did not break his legs. Because the Law of Moses required that the bones of the paschal lambs be unbroken, not breaking his legs indicated that he was indeed the Lamb of God. This is followed by a striking sign: "But one of the soldiers with a spear pierced his side, and forthwith came there out *blood and water*" (John 19:34, emphasis added).

Given the blood and water imagery in the Gospel of John, the blood and water that flowed from his side can represent some important truths about Jesus, truths emphasized by the presence of his mother. In this case, the blood signifies the mortality that he inherited from his mother, which gave him power to lay down his life as a sacrifice for sin (see John 10:17–18). The water, which Jesus earlier described as a well of water springing up into eternal life (John 4:14) and a river of living water (7:38), represents the divinity and immortality that he received from God, his Father. This blood and water imagery connects the Incarnation with his mortal death, reminding us that after God himself, there is no greater witness of Jesus Christ than his mother. No one else knows better the truth of his divine conception and miraculous birth, and no one probably felt more strongly the pain of his atoning death.

Meeting Jesus at the Empty Tomb

Mary Magdalene, who also stood at the foot of the cross as a witness to Jesus's death, is the first direct witness of his resurrection in John's Gospel. Others saw the empty tomb and the grave clothes, but she was the first to see the Risen Lord. In John's account, early on the first day of the week Mary came to the sepulcher and found the stone rolled away and the tomb empty. She hurried to tell Peter and the Beloved Disciple, who ran ahead of her to investigate the now-empty tomb. After they returned to where they were staying in the city, Mary was left at the tomb, alone and weeping (John 1:1–11). She then saw two angels sitting in the tomb, who asked her simply, "*Woman*, why weepest thou?" (John 20:13, emphasis added). Explaining that she fears that someone has stolen Jesus's body, she turned and saw Jesus but did not recognize him. According to John, Jesus asked her the same question, "*Woman*, why weepest thou?" (John 20:15, emphasis added). This double use of the greeting "Woman" (Greek, *gynai*) connects Mary with the mother of Lord, with other women in the Gospel of John, and, I would suggest, with women who follow Jesus in every age.[18]

For reasons that are not completely clear, Mary did not recognize Jesus when he first spoke to her. We do not know whether her vision was obscured by tears or foliage or whether somehow the resurrected Jesus looked different than he had in mortal life. When he called her by her name, however, she immediately recognized him and apparently fell at his feet or began to embrace him. Although the King James Version reads, "Jesus saith unto her, '*Touch me not*; for I am not yet ascended to my Father'" (John 20:17), the Greek text actually reads, "Do not keep touching me" or "Do not hold on to me" (Greek, *mē mou haptou*).[19] This conveys the impression that Mary, having found Jesus, was holding on to him and did not want to lose him again. Jesus, however, would need to ascend to the Father before long, while she must continue here and complete her mortal mission, a major part of which is to be a witness.[20]

This is evident in the commission that Jesus immediately gave Mary: "Go to my brethren, and say unto them, I ascend unto my Father, and your Father; and to my God, and your God" (John 20:17). Because the word *apostolos* means "one who was sent,"[21] Mary Magdalene has sometimes been called "the apostle to the apostles" (Latin, *apostolorum apostola*),[22] and she shared with the remaining eleven of the Twelve that she had seen, heard, and even touched the Lord.

Given how constrained women were in that time and culture, rarely being able to act without the approval of the men in their lives, the Lord's choice of her as his first witness after the Resurrection is striking. This historical window reveals a Jesus who was not constrained by many of the social mores and biases of his day. John's use of the generalizing term "woman" and the scriptures' silence regarding any other aspects of the relationship between Mary and Jesus encourage us to also use this as a mirror to our own discipleship. The Lord is not a respecter of persons, and all of us—women and men—can, and should, receive our own, personal testimony that he died for us and that he rose from the dead.[23]

Learning from Women Who Know

The mother of Jesus and Mary Magdalene serve as models for us of women who gained a sure knowledge that Jesus is the Son of God, that he can work miracles in our lives, that he died for us, and that he rose triumphantly from the tomb. They were like so many Latter-day Saint women today, who according to Julie B. Beck, general president of the Relief Society from 2007–2012, are "women who know and love the Lord and bear testimony of Him, women who are strong and immovable and who do not give up during difficult and discouraging times."[24] The apostle Paul spoke of this kind of testimony when he wrote to Timothy of "the unfeigned faith that is in thee, which dwelt first in thy grandmother Lois, and thy mother Eunice" (2 Timothy 1:5). While testimony comes from the Spirit, often the women of Christ who raise us, teach us, or share our lives with us are the ones who plant and nourish the seeds of faith. My own mother not only "told me the stories of Jesus" when I was a child; she showed me how to live his gospel by the way she lived. Now the steadfastness of my wife and the fervent belief of my daughter continue to strengthen my faith and motivate me to better follow Christ.

Yet sentimentality for parents or affection for others currently in our lives, male or female, is not enough. When others share what they know about Jesus Christ in their words and their deeds, their witness only takes root when we nurture it and then turn to the source of their faith. Indeed, it is not our witness or our example that is important but ultimately how we use these to help people come unto Christ. When Jesus taught the Nephites that he was the light of the world, he went on to say, "Behold I am the light which ye shall hold up—that which ye have seen me do" (3 Nephi 18:24). Like the mother of Jesus, we must magnify the Lord by finding ways to bring him more fully into this world. When we help others to follow him, saying "Whatsoever he saith unto you, do it" (John 2:5), we help bring faith and miracles into their lives. We can let both Marys bring us to the cross, weeping both in sorrow and gratitude, to see it not just as the means of Jesus's death but also the way by which he brings us eternal life. Like Mary Magdalene, we can wait in hope at the Empty Tomb, looking forward to the day when he will call us by name and our faith will become knowledge.

NOTES

1. There is some difficulty in reading John 19:25, which can be read to include four women (Jesus's mother, her sister, Mary the wife of Cleophas, and Mary Magdalene) or three (Jesus's mother, her sister who was Mary the wife of Cleophas, and Mary Magdalene). Because it is unlikely that two sisters in the same family would both be named Mary, the first possibility it more likely. See Brown, *Gospel according to John,* 904–6; Thompson, *John,* 399.
2. According to Josephus, women and slaves were not allowed to testify in court (*Antiquities of the Jews* 4.8.15 §219; Whiston, 156). Even in the twelfth century, Maimonides still maintained that according to Jewish law women were among ten classes not competent to attest or testify (Yad, Edut 9:1; see *Encyclopedia Judaica* under "witness"). While Greek women suffered similar legal disabilities (see Roger Just, *Women in Athenian Law and Life* [New York: Routledge, 1989], 33–36, 39), Roman women in general had more rights (see Jane F. Gardner, *Women in Roman Law and Society* [Bloomington and Indianapolis: Indiana University Press, 1986], 262–64).
3. Ritva H. Williams, "The Mother of Jesus at Cana: A Social-Science Interpretation of John 2:1–12," *Catholic Biblical Quarterly* 59.4 (1997): 679; Conway, *Men and Women in the Fourth Gospel*, 70.
4. Possibilities could include anyone from the Beloved Disciple if he were John the Zebedee (John's mother Salome and Jesus's mother Mary seem to have been sisters) to Nathanael (he was the last disciple called in ch. 1 and is identified as being from Cana in John 21:2), to a member of the Holy Family itself. See references cited in Huntsman, "Word Was Made Flesh," 55 n. 80.
5. David J. Williams, "Bride, Bridegroom," *Dictionary of Jesus and the Gospels*, 87.
6. Huntsman, *Miracles of Jesus*, 18.
7. The Greek *ti emoi kai soi* literally means, "What is this to me and you?" While some have seen frustration in his remarks by comparing it with a similar Hebrew phrase, *mah lî wālāk*, which is frequently used to connote sharpness in the Old Testament, or with parallels in the synoptic Gospels, where is appears on the desperate lips of the demon-possessed, the context here is different than any of these possible parallels. Jesus may simply have been asking how this was their family's concern. See the discussions and further references by Williams, "The Mother of Jesus at Cana," 686–88; Conway, *Men and Women in the Fourth Gospel*, 72; and Bennema, *Encountering Jesus*, 138.
8. Bennema, *Encountering Jesus*, 137–38.

9. Brown, *Gospel according to John*, 99; Leon Morris, *The Gospel according to John*, The New International Commentary on the New Testament, revised edition (Grand Rapids, Mich.: Eerdmans, 1995), 159–59.
10. For instance, see Talmage, *Jesus the Christ,* 136.
11. Huntsman, "Word Made Flesh," 56.
12. Huntsman, *Miracles of Jesus*, 16–19.
13. See Ether 3:8–9; see Leviticus 17:11–14; Ecclesiastes 14:19; 1 Corinthians 15:50. Joseph Fielding Smith wrote, "After the resurrection from the dead our bodies will be spiritual bodies, but they will be bodies that are tangible, bodies that have been purified, but they will nevertheless be bodies of flesh and bones . . . they will not be blood bodies, they will no longer be quickened by blood but quickened by the spirit which is eternal and they shall become immortal and shall never die" (*Conference Report*, April 1917, 63).
14. Huntsman, "Word Made Flesh," 55–57; *Miracles of Jesus*, 19.
15. Morris, *Gospel according to John*, 717–18; Bennema, *Encountering Jesus*, 142–43. This position does not account for the fact that she had other children, such as James and Jude, who should have been available to aid in her support.
16. Brown, *Gospel according to John*, 922–27; Morris, *Gospel according to John*, 718 n. 67; Conway, *Men and Women in the Fourth Gospel*, 80–85.
17. Huntsman, "Lamb of God," 54–55.
18. Eric D. Huntsman, *God So Loved the World: The Final Day of the Savior's Life* (Salt Lake City: Deseret Book, 2011), 114.
19. This is a present imperative in Greek, which in the negative has the connotation of stopping a continuous action rather than not doing something at all. Joseph Smith's inspired revision supports this translation, which reads "*Hold* me not" (JST John 20:17, emphasis added).
20. Huntsman, *God So Loved the World*, 114.
21. Bauer, "apostolos," *Greek-English Lexicon*, 122.
22. See Jane Schaberg, *The Resurrection of Mary Magdalene: Legends, Apocrypha, and the Christian Testament* (New York: Continuum, 2004), 88.
23. Huntsman, *God So Loved the World*, 114
24. Julie A. Beck, "Mothers Who Know," *Ensign* (November 2007): 78.

Chapter 3

Nicodemus

How Can These Things Be?

"Jesus answered and said unto him, Art thou a master of Israel, and knowest not these things? Verily, verily, I say unto thee, We speak that we do know, and testify that we have seen; and ye receive not our witness." (John 3:10–11)

Nicodemus is an intriguing character who appears three times in the Gospel of John, reflecting a different kind of experience than that of either the first disciples or the women who knew. Unlike the first disciples, who responded to the witness of others and then set out clearly on a path of discipleship, or the women, who appear in the narrative as already resolute followers, Nicodemus represents a different, more difficult path to belief.[1] Though attracted to Jesus because of the evidence of signs, Nicodemus still struggled to understand and accept what Jesus teaches him. Seemingly confused by his first encounter with the Lord (John 3:1–15), he recedes from the narrative, only to appear again in a contentious meeting of the Jewish leadership about how they should respond to Jesus. Here he came forward suggesting that they should give Jesus a fair hearing and try to understand him better, but his tentative efforts falter in the face of the opposition of his peers (John 7:45–53). Despite his hesitancy, Nicodemus nevertheless came forward after Jesus's crucifixion and joins Joseph of Arimathaea in giving the Lord an honorable burial, at last recognizing Jesus as the promised king of Israel (John 19:38–42).

This uneven trajectory has led commentators to differ on how to interpret Nicodemus's experience. Some see him as responding inadequately to Jesus, never evidencing enough faith to be considered someone who accepted Jesus and the salvation that he came to offer.[2] Others suggest that his nascent belief led him to be a secret disciple who at last came out in the open,[3] showing by his actions at Jesus's burial that he had at last developed saving faith.[4] Regardless of which position might be correct historically, as a character Nicodemus reflects the possibility of a type of discipleship with which many today may identify.[5] Sometimes we have a desire to believe, but our questions take us along a different path than others travel. We may struggle to understand what others accept more easily, looking for more evidence or trying to square gospel propositions with what we already accept or assume to be true. Sometimes we may be hesitant to embrace privately or proclaim publicly what we either suspect or want to be true. Still, though our path may be different than the paths others follow, when we come to know Jesus for ourselves, our discipleship can be no less genuine—and in the end, no less saving as long as we still come to Christ.

Nicodemus's Background and Interest in Jesus

Nicodemus's first appearance in John introduces a more developed, or "round," character than those met earlier in this Gospel. He is described as both a Pharisee and as "a ruler of the Jews" (John 3:1), with questions and responses that give us some insight into his thoughts and feelings. The Pharisees were a Jewish sect known for their devotion to the Law of Moses and the religious traditions of their people. The rulers of the Jews in John were the religious and civil elites in the official council known as the Sanhedrin, who tried to balance the interest of their people and the occupying power of the Romans. While the Sanhedrin was largely under the control of the chief priests and other Sadducees, leading Pharisees such as Nicodemus were also part of it. While the Gospel of John often portrays both these groups negatively, showing them as active opponents of Jesus, this does not mean that all Pharisees or Jewish leaders were either hypocritical or self-serving. Nicodemus, in fact, represents a well-educated, wealthy, and devout person who was genuinely seeking truth. Still, he is initially unable to understand it when Jesus teaches it to him.[6]

The episode before Nicodemus's first scene helps us better understand his motivation for his coming to Jesus. Jesus was in Jerusalem for the Passover and had already drawn attention to himself because of his actions in the temple, which he had publicly cleared of the merchants and moneychangers who had filled its outer courts (John 2:12–22). Because the Jewish leadership—whom John frequently refers to as "the Jews" (Greek, *hoi Ioudaioi*)—were well-versed in prophetic precedents,[7] they recognized that his actions were somehow a prophetic sign but failed to understand its meaning (John 2:18). When Jesus responded by comparing the future destruction of the temple with his own coming death, these leaders and Jesus's own disciples still did not understand what he meant (John 2:19–22). Despite this, many began to believe in Jesus because of the miraculous signs that he was performing (John 2:23), referring apparently to both miraculous acts like changing water into wine and symbolic acts such as his symbolic cleansing of the temple.[8] John certainly connects Nicodemus with this earlier group of Jewish believers when he writes, "The same came to Jesus by night, and said unto him, Rabbi, we know that thou art a teacher come from God: for no man can do these miracles that thou doest, except God be with him" (John 3:2).

This context provided John a chance to explain how well Jesus understands people like Nicodemus. The description of the temple incident closes with the observation, "But Jesus did not commit," or entrust, "himself unto them, because he knew all *men* . . . for he knew what was in *man*" (John 2:24–25, emphasis added). The word "man" here (Greek, *anthrōpos*) refers to any person, man or woman, so when John introduces Nicodemus as "a *man* of the Pharisees, named Nicodemus" (John 3:1), he may be generalizing his experience.[9] It also shows that Jesus knew Nicodemus and his motivations for coming to him, just as he knows each of us.

Misunderstanding Jesus

Despite Nicodemus's education and his incipient faith in Jesus, he repeatedly misunderstood what Jesus tried to teach him, illustrating that it is impossible to understand the things of God without the Spirit. Some interpreters have assumed that Nicodemus's coming to see Jesus at night indicates that he was trying to come secretly, so that the other Jewish leaders would not know of his interest in Jesus. Others have suggested that there may have been nothing surprising in his actions, because rabbis in the following period frequently held discussions with their students and fellow teachers in the evening.[10] Symbolically, however, coming by night appears to reflect Nicodemus's lack of understanding: he was "in the dark" about Jesus's real identity and mission, hearkening back to the prologue, which had taught that "the light shineth in the darkness; and the darkness comprehendeth it not" (John 1:5).

John frames this episode as a dialogue, a back-and-forth discussion between Nicodemus and Jesus that is the first of several such verbal exchanges between Jesus and characters in the Gospel of John. Such a format is engaging for us as readers, drawing us into the story and allowing us to feel like we are part of the conversation. Jesus's responses to Nicodemus show that he knows where

Nicodemus stands in terms of faith, while Nicodemus's subsequent questions reveal that he remains "in the dark," failing to understand the concepts that Jesus is trying to teach him. Jesus responds to Nicodemus's acknowledgment that Jesus is "a teacher come from God" with a series of declarations that will show that he is that and more: he is not just "come from God" in the sense that God approves of him. He has literally come down from heaven, and to understand that and prepare to go into heaven himself, Nicodemus, like all of us, must be become something different.

Jesus's first proposition to Nicodemus is one well known to Christians today: "Except a man *be born again*, he cannot see the kingdom of God" (John 3:3, emphasis added). What is translated as "be born again" (Greek, *gennēthȩ̄ anōthen*) literally means "born from above." Besides implying somehow being born a second time, this phrase also suggests the source and nature of the new birth. Like the Book of Mormon, which often prefers the expression "born of God" for being born again,[11] this new birth is intended to make us more like God, who is in heaven. Nicodemus, trying to understand this concept literally, fails to understand, replying in disbelief, "How can a man be born when he is old? can he enter the second time into his mother's womb, and be born?" (John 3:4).[12]

Jesus responded by declaring to Nicodemus, "Except a man be born of water and of the Spirit, he cannot enter into the kingdom of God" (John 3:5). We primarily use this passage to confirm that we need both water baptism and the sanctifying, transforming gift of the Holy Ghost. In its original context, however, Jesus's statement also calls upon Nicodemus to reflect more upon the nature of this new birth, which is heavenly, as opposed to our physical birth, which is "of the flesh," or earthly (John 3:6; see John 1:13). Seeing that Nicodemus is surprised or even astonished at this idea, Jesus explains that such matters must be understood by the Spirit, which comes upon us like the blowing wind that we feel even if we do not always understand where it comes from or where it is going (John

3:7–8). In other words, we can feel that something is right even if we do not always understand everything about it.

Nicodemus failed to understand how this is possible, perhaps expecting from his training to have more logical and less symbolic explanations of such vital truths. This earned what seems like a rather strong rebuke from Jesus: "Art thou a master of Israel, and knowest not these things?" (John 3:10). Though a teacher himself, Nicodemus was not able to understand what Jesus was teaching him, suggesting perhaps that those who rely too much on their own understanding sometimes fail to understand gospel truths. Misunderstanding Jesus, however, is not limited in the Gospel of John to the educated and well-off. Some of the Twelve and the Samaritan woman, who comes to faith in the next chapter more quickly than Nicodemus, will also initially fail to understand Jesus.[13]

"Even So Must the Son of Man Be Lifted Up"

Nicodemus's failure to understand was not limited to just a specific concept, such as the doctrine of the new birth. Rather, he failed to grasp that there was a different way of learning truth. Jesus explained to him, "Verily, verily, I say unto thee, We speak that we do *know*, and testify that we have *seen*; and ye receive not our witness" (John 3:11, emphasis added). When Jesus and others taught of what they know, it was because they had "seen"—that is, they had gained knowledge from actual experience. By shifting from the singular, "thee," to the plural, "ye," in John 3:11, Jesus indicated that Nicodemus was not alone in having difficulty understanding these kinds of spiritual matters. While Nicodemus may well have represented a particular historical group of teachers and leaders at the time of Jesus, he also symbolized many of us who struggle to have faith when we fail to understand that some questions can only be answered through spiritual means.[14]

In the case of Jesus, he had seen and known the things of God because he had actually come down from heaven (John 3:13). Because a testimony of Jesus and what he came to do is the key to salvation, this is what Nicodemus, and each of us, must come to know through the Spirit. Jesus ended his discussion with Nicodemus with this striking prophecy: "And as Moses lifted up the serpent in the wilderness, *even so must the Son of man be lifted up*: That whosoever believeth in him should not perish, but have eternal life" (John 3:14–15, emphasis added). Nicodemus would have recognized the reference to the Old Testament story of the fiery serpents whose bites were only healed when the children of Israel looked toward the brass serpent that Moses had raised up on a pole (see Numbers 21:4–9). What he does not seem to have comprehended is that just as Jesus came down from heaven, so he would return, being lifted up in the process of preparing the way back for all of us.

"Being lifted up" has two meanings in John's Gospel. Explicitly it refers to Jesus's being lifted up on the cross. Implicitly it extends to his ascension to heaven, as when he tells Mary Magdalene, "I ascend unto my Father, and your Father; to my God, and your God" (John 20:17). The Risen Lord taught this to the Nephites after his resurrection when he declared to them, "And my Father sent me that I might be lifted up upon the cross; and after that I had been lifted up upon the cross, that I might draw all men unto me, that as I have been lifted up by men even so should men be lifted up by the Father, to stand before me, to be judged of their works . . ." (3 Nephi 27:14). This is the heart of the gospel message, and reflecting upon this leads John to reflect, "For God so loved the world, that he gave his only begotten Son, that whosoever believeth in him should not perish, but have everlasting life. For

God sent not his Son into the world to condemn the world; but that the world through him might be saved" (John 3:16–17).[15]

Hesitant Belief

Although Nicodemus did not understand Jesus at their first meeting, he nevertheless continued to view Jesus favorably and felt that Jesus should at least be given a fair hearing. When Jesus later delivered a powerful discourse in the temple that caused many to begin to believe on him, it led the Jerusalem leadership to resolve that they must arrest him (John 7:32). When the officers whom they sent failed to take him into custody, the chief priests and Pharisees held a meeting to decide what to do about Jesus. In it, Nicodemus tentatively came forward, suggesting that the council should at least hear Jesus before it judged him. Nevertheless, when his suggestion was met with derision and the possible suggestion that Nicodemus was himself one of Jesus's followers, Nicodemus did not try to defend Jesus further (John 7:45–53).[16]

When John introduces Nicodemus again in this scene, he emphasizes that Nicodemus was the one "who came to Jesus by night" (John 7:50). This reminds us that in his first meeting with Jesus, Nicodemus had "been in the dark," not understanding the Lord's words. Without a firm conviction, Nicodemus flags in his support of Jesus, representing those of us who, not yet having a firm testimony of Christ, may be hesitant in our own belief. Often we can accept the basic facts about Jesus in a general way, allowing us to continue as members of the Church out of tradition, family loyalty, or convenience. However, when strong opposition rises or arguments emerge against what we think or simply hope is true, we may falter. Or, like those in Lehi's dream, sometimes those who partake of the fruit are later overwhelmed by mists of darkness or become ashamed in the face of the opposition of the world, leading them to leave the path (see 1 Nephi 8:20–28). Still, the story of

Nicodemus is not over yet, nor is it for any of us in those moments when we might hesitate in our belief.

HONORING JESUS AT HIS BURIAL

Nicodemus's final appearance in the Gospel of John occurs after the Crucifixion. When Joseph of Arimathea, who is described as "a disciple of Jesus, but secretly for fear of the Jews," obtained from Pilate the body of Jesus (John 19:38), Nicodemus joined him in giving it a proper burial. Nicodemus brought a surprisingly large amount of spices, about seventy-five pounds by modern measure, to prepare the body.[17] He and Joseph completed their task before sundown, when the Sabbath began. Some commentators argue that the two only performed this final service for Jesus out of a general respect for the dead and from a desire to keep the Sabbath and Passover festival from being defiled. The kingly amount of spices that Nicodemus brought—far more than required for an honorable burial—suggests otherwise. Having previously only come to Jesus at night or having hesitantly spoken for him in closed council, Nicodemus now came out in the open in his acceptance of Jesus as the true King of Israel.[18] While Nicodemus at this dark moment may not have understood that Jesus would soon rise from the dead, he, like Mary of Bethany who had anointed Jesus in preparation of his death and burial (John 12:1–8; see chapter 6 below), stepped forward to act in love and devotion.[19]

The reason for this change seems to be that Nicodemus at last saw in Jesus's crucifixion what he meant when he spoke of being lifted up like the serpent in the wilderness (see John 3:14–15). Indeed, Jesus later told a crowd in Jerusalem, "When ye have lifted up the Son of man, then shall ye know that I am he . . ." (John 8:28). Seeing Jesus raised up on the cross may have been the ultimate sign for Nicodemus, the powerful image of the Son of God being sacrificed for his people finally overcoming his previous lack of understanding. Nicodemus's earlier, hesitant steps may contrast with the path of others in the Gospel of John, but eventually he arrives at a similar point of faith, an important reminder to us that different paths of discipleship can lead to the same end.

THE CHALLENGES OF DIFFERENT KINDS OF FAITH

The example of Nicodemus reminds us that we must be careful about judging the spiritual journeys of other people. Sometimes we can be too quick to judge the faith of others, faulting them for questioning or perhaps insisting that people testify that they "know" when sometimes what is important is just believing or having the desire to believe (see Alma 32:26–27). The story of Nicodemus, in fact, sometimes reminds me of my own experience, helping me remember when I have leaned too much on my own understanding or when I let otherwise real questions become so large that I failed to see anything else. I have learned that it is possible to have questions and concerns but still hold fast to the important truths that Jesus is the Son of God, that he suffered and died for us, that he rose from the dead, and that this is his Church.

One of those times occurred in the middle of my service in the Thailand Bangkok Mission. I was working in the mission office and was outwardly an enthusiastic and fervent missionary. Always eager to study the scriptures but perhaps with too much of a need for rigidly rational explanations, I had become distracted with the historical interpretation of certain passages of scripture that my fellow missionaries regularly used as proof texts—that is, as passages that prove the point we are trying to make. Trying to understand the issues intellectually, I failed to understand that there could be more than one legitimate interpretation of the passages I was concerned about, and these included the traditional meanings that my fellow missionaries held. Letting my concerns grow unchecked, I even began to question my entire testimony.

In the midst of this personal turmoil, the mission president asked me to offer our usual morning devotional in his office. The passage I chose to share was Ether 4:13–16, in which Moroni wrote of the great things that we sometimes fail to see because of unbelief. His injunctions to "rend that veil of unbelief" and "call upon the Father in my name with a broken heart and a contrite spirit" reduced me to tears, leading President Weed to excuse the other elders. Coming around his desk to sit beside me, he put his arm around me as I confessed to my shaken faith and tried to explain all the intellectual arguments that had so occupied me. He neither corrected me nor told me that I was wrong to question; in fact, he told me that it was good and that he wanted me to think for myself. However, he also shared a scripture that has since become a touchstone for me when I find myself in similar situations: "But to be learned is good if they hearken unto the counsels of God" (2 Nephi 9:29). Like Nicodemus, I needed to realize that some things could only be learned from the Spirit, and like that teacher of old, I needed to center my faith solely in Christ and his Atonement.

Since that time, I have found a course of discipleship that works for me, balancing a desire for knowledge with a trust in God even when I do not understand. Nonetheless, that experience, together with meeting a wide variety of differently believing people over the years, has sensitized me to the fact there are many different kinds of faith. Some of us are blessed with simple, unquestioning faith. That is a great gift, especially if it does not lead to being critical of others who are more questioning or who take longer to come to similar conclusions. However, this simple approach can sometimes lead to what biblical scholar Craig Evans calls "brittle fundamentalism," a rigidity that can lead to a collapse of faith when certain assumptions do not sustain later examination.[20]

On the other hand, those who by nature need to question almost everything may seem to be in a constant state of mental or emotional tension too. Yet Terryl and Fiona Givens have noted that what Fyodor Dostoevsky called "the crucible of doubt" can also lead to a mature, deep faith that is accompanied by rich empathy for the questioning of others.[21] With these different approaches and others in between, we may find that the challenge is not in the different kinds of discipleship that people experience as we travel to the same goal. Rather it is found in the way we treat others whose faith is different from our own. Whether we are an Andrew, Peter, Nathanael, either of the Marys, Nicodemus, or someone completely different, we can all still be beloved disciples if we earnestly believe in him and try to follow Jesus Christ.

NOTES

1. Culpepper, *Anatomy of the Fourth Gospel*, 134–36.
2. Conway, *Men and Women in the Fourth Gospel*, 85–86, 103; Culpepper, *Anatomy of the Fourth Gospel*, 146.
3. Brown, *Gospel according to John*, 2.959–60.
4. Rudolph Schnackenburg, *The Gospel according to John* (New York: Crossroad, 1990), 1.364–65; Morris, *Gospel according to John*, 825–26.
5. Raymond Collins, "Representative Figures," *These Things Have Been Written: Studies on the Fourth Gospel* (Louvain Theological & Pastoral Monographs 2; Grand Rapids, Mich.: Eerdmans, 1990), 15.
6. Conway, *Men and Women in the Fourth Gospel*, 88–91; Bennema, *Encountering Jesus*, 148–49.
7. The identity of this group and John's use of the term *hoi Ioudaioi*, or "the Jews," will be discussed in more detail in chapter 5.
8. Craig R. Koester, "Theological Complexity and the Characterization of Nicodemus in John' Gospel," *Characters and Characterization in the Gospel of John*, ed. Christopher W. Skinner, Library of New Testament Studies 461 (New York: Bloomsbury, 2013), 170–71.
9. Conway, *Men and Women in the Fourth Gospel*, 88–91; Bennema, *Encountering Jesus*, 148–49.
10. Conway, *Men and Women in the Fourth Gospel*, 92–93; Bennema, *Encountering Jesus*, 150–51.

11. See, for example, see Mosiah 27:25, 38; Alma 5:14; 22:15; 36:5, 23–26; 38:6.
12. Conway, *Men and Women in the Fourth Gospel*, 97–98.
13. Conway, *Men and Women in the Fourth Gospel*, 98; Koester, "Theological Complexity and the Characterization of Nicodemus," 168.
14. Koester, "Theological Complexity and the Characterization of Nicodemus," 169.
15. Commentators debate where Jesus's words to Nicodemus end and where the narrator's reflection begins, but the shift to third person seems to support that this is, in fact, the inspired testimony of the author of Gospel of John. See Morris, *Gospel according to John*, 228, and Brown, *Gospel according to John*, 147–48.
16. Bennema, *Encountering Jesus*, 152–54.
17. Brown, *Gospel according to John*, 2.941.
18. Brown, *Gospel according to John*, 2.969; Koester, "Theological Complexity and the Characterization of Nicodemus," 177–79.
19. Koester, "Theological Complexity and the Characterization of Nicodemus," 178–80.
20. Craig A. Evans, *Fabricating Jesus* (Downers Grove, Ill.: IVP Books, 2006), 19–21, 25–31.
21. Terryl and Fiona Givens, *The Crucible of Doubt: Reflections on the Quest for Faith* (Salt Lake City: Deseret Book, 2014), vi, and their own examples that include 10, 36, 117–19, 126–130, 137–140, 143–145.

CHAPTER 4

THE WOMAN AT THE WELL

Drinking the Waters of Life with the Woman of Samaria

"But whosoever drinketh of the water that I shall give him shall never thirst; but the water that I shall give him shall be in him a well of water springing up into everlasting life." (John 4:14)

The Samaritan woman—the central character of John 4—provides a ready contrast with Nicodemus, and she compares favorably with the mother of Jesus and Mary Magdalene.[1] While Nicodemus had sought out Jesus, albeit rather secretly at night, Jesus himself arranged to meet the Samaritan woman in the middle of the day. Nicodemus was a man of status and education as well as a Jewish leader in the Jerusalem establishment, whereas the woman was on the social and economic margins of her own reviled ethnic community.[2] He was a respected "teacher in Israel," but she had a questionable marital history that branded her a sinner in her community. Nicodemus asked a series of questions but failed to understand Jesus's answers. The Samaritan woman, on the other hand, engaged in a longer, mutual dialogue with Jesus, one that led her to greater spiritual understanding and quickly brought her to saving faith in Jesus as the Messiah.[3] Although she started out knowing nothing about Jesus, she became a disciple. She then became "a woman who knew" like the mother of Jesus and Mary Magdalene,[4] and this testimony helped bring her entire community to a knowledge of the truth. As a named character, Nicodemus was tied to a specific historical individual and context. The Samaritan woman, on the other hand, like other unnamed characters in John, is one with which readers can often more easily identify.

Consequently, the Samaritan woman's path of faith can serve as a ready template for those who come to know Jesus and accept him as their Savior. Whenever, wherever, and however we come to meet the Lord, we can all learn who he really is and accept the life he offers us. What is particularly powerful about the Samaritan woman's experience is that her role as an outsider underscores that Jesus came for *everyone* regardless of race, ethnic background, gender, or lifestyle. In this regard, Jesus is a disruptor of categories and social conventions. While our paths to Jesus might vary greatly, we can still walk the same road with him. Indeed, as the apostle Paul taught, "There is neither Jew nor Greek, there is neither bond nor free, there is neither male nor female: for ye are all one in Christ Jesus" (Galatians 3:28).

Jews and Samaritans, Men and Women

When Jesus sat down by a well near a Samaritan village called Sychar (John 4:4–6),[5] a number of historical, religious, and cultural factors had the potential of complicating his interactions with the Samaritan woman who came there to draw water. Samaria was the mountainous region between Galilee in the north, where Jesus grew up and spent most of his ministry, and Judea and Jerusalem to the south. Settled by the tribes of Ephraim and Manasseh, Samaria formed the heartland of the northern kingdom of Israel when the United Kingdom was divided after Solomon's death about 930 BC.

The name "Samaria" came from the name of the final and most important capital of the kingdom, which Omri had built about 876 BC (1 Kings 16:24). Throughout the course of its independent history in the Old Testament, the northern kingdom had frequently fallen into apostasy. Sometimes the northern tribes strayed into worshiping pagan gods, such as the Canaanite storm god Bā'al or the fertility goddess Asherah. Yet even when the northern tribes worshiped *YHWH*, or Jehovah, they often did so in the wrong way and at the wrong places, at shrines such as the ones at Dan in the north or Bethel in the south rather than at the temple in Jerusalem.

Historically, this apostasy led to the destruction of the northern kingdom of Israel when it lost the protection of the Lord. In 721 BC the Assyrian Empire conquered Israel and destroyed its capital at Samaria, deporting most of its inhabitants.[6] The Assyrians then brought at least five groups of foreign peoples into the region to replace those who been deported, settling them in a colony on the site of the old city of Samaria. Here, and perhaps in other urban centers, these settlers might have mixed with some of the remaining Israelites. They then worshiped not only their own gods but also accepted Jehovah as "the god of the land" (2 Kings 17:24–33). Later, when Alexander the Great conquered the Holy Land in 332 BC, he established a new Greek-speaking colony at the site of Samaria, which was later substantially rebuilt as a Roman-style city by Herod the Great. The mixed heritage and religion of those in the city of Samaria seems to have prompted some Jewish writers, like the historian Josephus and the later authors of the Talmud, a compilation and commentary on Jewish law, to view all the inhabitants of the region as being of mixed blood and questionable Israelite religion.[7]

In the villages of the countryside, however, the population consisted of the remnants of the original tribes of Ephraim and Manasseh, who continued to worship Jehovah, the god of their ancestors, but in a way that caused them to differ religiously from the Jews when they returned from their own exile in Babylonia. When the Jews began rebuilding Jerusalem and the temple, these Israelite Samaritans offered to help, but their offer was rejected (see Ezra 4:1–3). Instead, after a period of mixed interactions with the Jews of Jerusalem, they built their own temple on Mount Gerizim,[8] which had been the mount of blessing when the children of Israel had entered the Holy Land (see Deuteronomy 11:29; 27:11–13; Joshua 8:33). This became a point of contention between the Jews and the Samaritans, and sometime between 128 and 110 BC, the Jewish leader John Hyrcanus destroyed the temple on Mount Gerizim. This led to increasing hostility on both sides, and religious differences added to the antipathy between the two groups. For instance, the Samaritans only accepted the five books attributed to Moses and rejected the prophetic and other books that the Jews accepted as scripture.[9] By the time of Jesus, ritual differences had led most Jews to see the Samaritans as unclean and not really Israelites.[10] However, Samaria itself remained part of the Land of Israel so that food grown there and water drawn from its wells was still ritually acceptable.

Gender was another complicating factor in Jesus's encounter with the woman of Samaria. Although many of the specific cultural restrictions that existed between men and women are mostly attested from later evidence in the rabbinic period,[11] like other conservative cultures in the ancient world, Jews and Samaritans at the time of Jesus would have been wary of direct interactions between a man and a woman who were not related. Because Jesus's disciples had left him at the well to go into the town to buy food (KJV, "meat"), Jesus and the woman would have been alone, which accentuated the perceived cultural impropriety. In addition, a Jewish purity regulation of AD 65–66, just over thirty years from the time of Jesus's ministry, warns of the permanent ritual impurity of Samaritan women,[12] making the narrator's threefold repetition of the phrase "woman of Samaria" (John 4:7, 9) a mark of double contempt.[13] Further, given that in the Old Testament wells were places where well-known men in the scriptural record found wives, Jesus's being alone with the woman there was potentially awkward. Abraham's servant, for instance, met Rebekah, who would become the wife of Abraham's son Isaac, at a well (Genesis 24:10–51), just as Jacob and Moses met their wives Rachel and Zipporah at wells (Genesis 29:1–14; Exodus 2:15–22). Because these earlier well scenes led to betrothals, the motif raises certain expectations in this episode that play out differently than anticipated. Rather than resulting in marriage, the Samaritan woman's meeting with Jesus resulted in her entering into a covenant relationship with him when she accepted him as her Messiah and Lord.[14]

Water Springing up to Everlasting Life

Despite these historical, religious, and cultural complications, Jesus seems to have deliberately chosen to meet this particular Samaritan woman at this specific spot. The Gospel of John carefully establishes the setting of Jesus's meeting with the woman, noting that as Jesus was returning to Galilee from Judea, "he must needs go through Samaria" (John 4:4). Although this verse seems to imply that the route itself was necessary, it was often not the preferred nor necessarily fastest way to travel from Jerusalem to Galilee. Not only did religiously scrupulous Jews prefer avoiding any contact with Samaritans, the more indirect course through the Jordan valley was in many ways an easier road because it avoided the rugged terrain of the Ephraim hill country.[15] On the other hand, the Gospel of John often uses the expression "must" in regard to necessary parts of Jesus's mission (see, for example, John 3:14, 30; 9:4; 10:16; 12:34; and 20:9).[16] Additionally, although Jesus in John rarely shows weakness or human need, in this scene he exhibits weariness and thirst primarily as a way of arranging for him to meet the woman. He sits by the well while his disciples go into the town to buy food and then asks the woman for a drink when she arrives (John 4:6–7). Nonetheless, he never drinks water from the well or eats of the food that his disciples bring when they return. In other words, it was out of divine necessity, or according to God's plan, that Jesus went through Samaria and stopped at that very well, perhaps with the intent that he meet this woman alone and then, through her, be introduced to the others in her village.

The conversation that ensues is longer, more involved, and more productive than Jesus's earlier conversation with Nicodemus. Whereas Nicodemus's interchange with Jesus consisted of a few exchanges that left him uncertain and unconverted, the Samaritan woman's conversation entailed several more questions and answers that led to steadily increasing understanding and faith.[17] In fact, this is one of the few instances where a dialogue between Jesus and a character does not turn into a monologue by the Lord or a theological reflection by the narrator. Indeed, the Samaritan woman in chapter 4 and Martha in chapter 11 represent the most productive, almost equal interchanges between Jesus and another speaker.[18] Jesus meets her at noon, much as Jacob had met Rachel at midday, (Genesis 29:7), an unusual hour because women usually drew water either at dawn or the early evening.[19] As the story unfolds, it becomes apparent that the woman may have come at this uncommon time to avoid other women or because they had shunned her,[20] but the overall reason seems to be symbolic. Unlike Nicodemus, who came secretly at night, the Samaritan woman came in the middle of the day, perhaps emphasizing the difference between those who love darkness and those who seek light, as mentioned in John 3:20–21.

Jesus's first comment to her is a strong request, set in the imperative, "Give me to drink." This surprises the woman, who replies, "How is it that thou, being a Jew, askest drink of me, which am a woman of Samaria?" (John 4:7–9).[21] The narrator further explains her surprise, noting "the Jews have no dealings with the Samaritans," which probably actually meant "use nothing in common" (Greek, *synchrōntai*). That is because if she, as a Samaritan woman, was considered ritually impure, she would have conveyed that impurity to the otherwise pure water that she drew through the jar that she used.[22] Therefore, by breaking social conventions by asking the Samaritan woman for a drink, in a single request Jesus rejected the ethnic, religious, and gender divisions that existed between them.[23]

Jesus's second comment immediately reveals that the purpose of his request had not been primarily to satisfy his thirst. Instead, he declared, "If thou knewest the gift of God, and who it is that saith to thee, Give me to drink; thou wouldest have asked of him, and he would have given thee living water" (John 4:10). His use of the phrase "living water" (Greek, *hydōr zōn*) is ambiguous. On the one hand, it could mean flowing water like that from a spring rather than the flat, stale water stored in cisterns or perhaps pooled in deep wells.[24] On the other hand, it could refer specifically to flowing water that was ritually pure in a Jewish context.[25] While the latter might have been ironic given the woman's presumed ritual impurity, the woman seems to have had the former in mind when she replies that Jesus had nothing to draw with and the well was deep. The traditional site of this episode is, in fact, an ancient well that is one hundred feet deep. Located near the foot of the sacred Mount Gerizim, it was near the site of Shechem, which was closely associated with Jacob in the Old Testament (Genesis 33:18; 48:22).[26]

Jesus's third comment, however, plays upon a possible third meaning of the expression "living water," at least the way it is expressed in John's Greek. While meaning flowing or ritually pure water in a Jewish context, the participle "living" (Greek, *zōn*) might convey the idea of water that gives or imparts life.[27] This seems to be the meaning implied by Jesus in his declaration, "Whosoever drinketh of this water shall thirst again: But whosoever drinketh of the water that I shall give him shall never thirst; but the water that I shall give him shall be in him *a well of water springing up into everlasting life*" (John 4:13–14, emphasis added). The Greek word that Jesus used for "well" in verse 14, *pēgē*, is the same one used when the well was introduced in verse 4 and literally means "spring" (in Hebrew, *'ayin*). On the other hand, both times the woman referred to the well in verses 11 and 12, she uses a word that means a common well (Greek, *phrear*) but which can also refer to a cistern, or place to store water (in Hebrew, *be'ēr*).[28] While the word used by the woman probably matches the actual well more directly, the word used by Jesus points to greater symbolic significance. First, it may allude to a story told in the Palestinian Targum—an Aramic translation and expansion of the Hebrew Bible—which tells that when Jacob met Rachel at a well in Haran, he lifted a stone off of a well, from which water *flowed* for twenty years.[29] In addition, in the Old Testament, *YHWH*, or Jehovah, was both a "fountain of life" (Psalm 36:9) and a "spring of living waters" (see Jeremiah 2:13; 17:13). In the Book of Mormon, Nephi similarly describes Jesus as the tree of life, or the love of God, and as "the fountain of living waters" (1 Nephi 11:25).[30]

"I PERCEIVE THAT THOU ART A PROPHET"

Apparently attracted to the idea of being freed from the laborious task of coming daily to draw water, the woman immediately responded to Jesus's offer of living water by saying, "Sir, give me this water, that I thirst not, neither come hither to draw" (John 4:15). When the woman thus fails to understand the import of what he was offering to her, Jesus shifts the conversation to a discussion of his identity.[31] When his fourth comment was an invitation to call her husband, she responded that she did not have a husband. Jesus responds, "Thou hast well said, I have no husband: For thou hast had five husbands; and he whom thou now hast is not thy husband" (John 4:17–18). It appears that Jews in this period were only allowed three marriages, so if the Samaritans followed similar customs, the woman's five marriages would have been scandalous.[32] This might explain why she came alone at an unusual time to draw water.[33] Stunned at Jesus's knowledge of her personal life, she replies simply, "Sir, I perceive that thou art a prophet" (John 4:19).

Though Jesus prophetically revealed details about the woman's personal life, his purpose was not to pass judgment. Instead, his revelation allowed him to comment on the nature of Samaritan worship and also to show that he knew her doings and heart as he earlier had with Nathanael.[34] Because there were five books attributed to Moses in the Old Testament, some commentators have suggested that the failure of the woman's five marriages might have symbolized that these Israelite Samaritans had failed to keep the Law of Moses in the past. By this interpretation, her current unlawful relationship reflected that they were not properly keeping it now. Others have noted that the number of her husbands was the same as the number of the gods of the five pagan nations that were supposedly the ancestors of the Samaritans. Under this interpretation, the five former husbands could represent the former relationship of the Samaritans to their pagan gods, and the man she was living with improperly now represented the illegitimate nature of the Samaritan worship of Jehovah. However, while 2 Kings 17:30–31 mentions the five nations who were brought in as urban colonists, it actually lists seven different ancestral gods.[35] Besides, we have noted that these were, in all probability, the ancestors of the gentile Samaritans, not of the Israelite Samaritans of the countryside.

Instead, because the Hebrew prophets frequently used marriage to describe the covenant relationship between Jehovah and his people, the woman's five failed marriages might represent the frequent apostasy of the northern tribes. As Sherri Brown, an assistant professor of New Testament at Creighton University, has noted, "Audiences might remember that Hosea, the prophet to the northern kingdom, primarily used the language of marriage, and broken marriage, to speak of the northern kingdom's covenant relationship with God and what he considered its breach of that covenant. Thus, Jesus is also articulating the current broken state of the Samaritans' relationship."[36] Interestingly, *Bā'al* is both the name of the pagan Canaanite storm god most frequently worshiped by the northern kingdom *and* the common term used by a woman for her husband. Accordingly, Jesus's reference to the Samaritan woman's "husbands" could still be a type of her Israelite ancestors' repeated dalliance with paganism.[37] Though the Samaritans of Jesus's day no longer worshiped Bā'al or any other pagan deity, Jesus's fellow Jews still maintained that the Samaritans were not in the correct covenant relationship with Jehovah.

Either because she understood the direction in which Jesus was moving their conversation or because she thought that as a prophet he could answer her questions, the woman raised one of the greatest points that continued to divide Samaritans and Jews. While her people strove to worship the Lord on Mount Gerizim, the Jews insisted that proper worship only took place on the temple mount in Jerusalem. When she asked about this, Jesus taught that worship is not so much about a place as it is the *object*, the Father, and the *means*, the spirit by which he is worshiped. While the King James translation explains that this is because "God is a Spirit" (4:24), the Greek phrase here, *pneuma ho theos*, can just as easily be rendered as "God is spirit," as it is in many modern translations. According to biblical scholar Raymond Brown, Jesus's description of God as spirit "is not an essential description of God, but is a description of God's dealings with men," as is the case in the letter of 1 John when God is similarly described as "God is light" or "God is love" (1 John 1:5; 4:8).[38] Similarly, when Jesus said, "salvation is of the Jews," he may not so much have been contrasting the worship of the Jews and the Samaritans as he was indicating that he himself, the source of salvation, came through the line of David, who was of the tribe of Judah. Taken together, these ideas can reflect our own understanding that, strictly speaking, we worship the Father in the name of the Son, who was God's means of bringing salvation to us, by the power of the Holy Ghost.

The woman's response to Jesus's pronouncements on worship is to testify, "I know that Messias cometh, which is called Christ: when he is come, he will tell us all things" (John 4:25). Rather than awaiting an anointed king of the lineage of David, the Samaritans looked forward to a "prophet like Moses" (Deuteronomy 18:15), whom they called the *ta'eb*, or "successor." Literally "the one who returns," this messianic prophet would reveal God's will just as Moses had.[39] Recognizing the validity of this messianic expectation, Jesus's seventh and final comment is the declaration, "I that speak unto thee *am he*" (John 4:26, emphasis added). Directly translated "I Am [is] the one speaking to you," this is the first time that the important Greek phrase *egō eimi* appears in John.[40] In the mouth of Jesus, *egō eimi* is important because it is the way the Septuagint had translated the divine name in Hebrew, *'ehyeh 'ašer 'ehyeh*, or "I Am that I Am," by which Jehovah revealed himself to Moses (Exodus 3:14). In other words, in the same statement Jesus identifies himself to the woman as both the prophetic Messiah she had been expecting and as Jehovah himself.

As their conversation progressed in this dialogue, the epithet "Samaritan" is dropped, but Jesus continues to refer to her as "woman," suggesting that a woman can be not just a fitting conversation partner but also a suitable disciple. With this knowledge of who Jesus is, the woman is now able to accept Jesus and thereby come into a correct, more full relationship with him and through him, with the Father. When the woman accepted Jesus, the betrothal motif suggested by the well imagery might reflect a symbolic marriage as her individual acceptance of Jesus led to her entering a covenant relationship with the Lord.[41] Neither her gender, nor her ethnicity, nor her past life could keep her—or can keep any of us—from becoming part of the body of Christ. As the Church, we are the bride, and he is the bridegroom.

A RICH HARVEST IN SAMARIA

At that moment, Jesus's disciples returned, surprised that he was breaking social conventions by talking alone with a woman.[42] The woman, on the other hand, "left her water pot, and went her way into the city" (John 4:28). Neither she nor Jesus had ever drunk any water from the well, but with her spiritual thirst quenched, she now felt a mission to share the living waters with the people of her town,[43] the very people who might have shunned and marginalized her for her marital history. However, leaving her water jar indicates more than simply her no longer needing the water of the well—leaving it behind is analogous to male disciples leaving behind their nets and other possessions when called to follow Jesus in the synoptic Gospels.[44] Likewise, her mission to bring others to Jesus parallels the first disciples, who brought friends, relatives, and others to him in the opening chapter of John. Indeed, her invitation, "Come, see a man, which told me all things that ever I did: is not this the Christ?" (John 4:29), echoes that of Jesus's call to Andrew and the other disciple and then Philip's invitation to Nathanael, "Come and see" (John 1:39, 46).

Disregarding the food that his disciples brought him, Jesus said that the fields were "white already to harvest" (John 4:35), a phrase and image that has become important in Restoration scripture to connote a rich missionary harvest (see D&C 4:4, 35; 6:3; 11:3; 12:3; 14:3; 33:3, 7). As the Samaritans from the village come out to meet Jesus in response to the woman's witness, Jesus explained to his disciples that they were about to reap her missionary efforts

(John 4:37–38). Significantly, the testimony that she had sown grows to full fruition when they hear the words of Jesus for themselves, "Now we believe, not because of thy saying: for we have heard him ourselves, and know that this is indeed the Christ, *the Saviour of the world*" (John 4:42, emphasis added). This is, in fact, the only time that this title, "the Savior of the world" is attested in the mortal ministry of Jesus.[45] As Colleen Conway, Professor of Religious Studies at Seton Hall University, has observed, "The woman moves from a mere conversation partner to a partner in Jesus's ministry . . . as the mother of Jesus is the co-worker of the Father, so the Samaritan woman becomes an indispensable co-worker of Jesus."[46] Marginalized by society as a woman, spurned by Jews as a Samaritan, and perhaps rejected by her own Samaritan community as a sinner, this woman showed that although salvation might have been "of the Jews," it was meant not only for the Jews and her fellow Samaritans but for the whole world.

EMBRACING THOSE WHO ARE DIFFERENT

Characters that play positive roles in the Gospel of John, such as the Samaritan woman, often exhibit initial shortcomings in both faith and understanding.[47] Yet, as is the case for each of us, when they encountered Jesus, they needed to make the choice to hear, accept, and the follow him. Similarly, when the Lord comes into our lives, we must make the decision to open our minds and hearts to him. This woman, an outsider who becomes an insider, became a model disciple by responding in faith and then actively bringing others to Jesus.[48] Clearly, it is significant that the first truly successful missionary in John is not someone that people in that time and culture would have either expected *or* respected. Likewise, today we must often set aside our expectations and our own biases to let Jesus be the Savior for *all* the world. As we become a worldwide church, we must be more willing and more openhearted to embrace those who are different, not just in other countries and in other cultures but often even in our own homes and communities.

A powerful parallel to the Samaritan woman in our dispensation is Jane Manning James (1813–1908), a faithful member of the Church who was of African descent. Not long after she heard Mormon elders preach in 1842, she joined the Church. That same year she led eight members of her family whom she had introduced to the gospel on a journey of over eight hundred miles from Wilton, Connecticut, to Nauvoo, Illinois—much of it on foot—in order to gather with the Latter-day Saints. In her autobiography, she recalled, "We walked until our shoes were worn out, and our feet became sore and cracked open and bled until you could see the whole print of our feet with blood on the ground. We stopped and united in prayer to the Lord; we asked God the Eternal Father to heal our feet and our prayers were answered and our feet were healed forthwith." She was in one of the first companies of pioneers to enter the Salt Lake Valley in 1847 and remained faithful throughout her life, even though her husband later left her and she was denied the temple blessings she sought during her mortal life, not being endowed by proxy until 1978.[49] Still, through her baptism and faithful membership, she, like the Samaritan woman, entered into a covenant relationship with the Lord, and in the end, she received all promised blessings. Her example of persistent faith has become more important today, not only for members of African descent but for all of us who can be inspired by her continued devotion in the face of adversity and systemic prejudice.[50]

President M. Russell Ballard, a member of the Twelve since 1985 and acting president of that quorum since 2018, taught, "We need to embrace God's children compassionately and eliminate any prejudice, including racism, sexism, and nationalism. Let it be said that we truly believe the blessings of the restored gospel of Jesus Christ are for every child of God."[51] In addition to reaching out to and loving others regardless of their gender, race, religion, orientation, or other background, we should also recognize those who have made different choices or made mistakes as our sisters and brothers. For instance, while we may sometimes be critical when we detect the smell of smoke or alcohol on someone who comes to church on Sunday morning, God is pleased that that person is there. He welcomes saints and sinners as long as they receive his Son, Jesus, and desire to follow him. In reality, we are all both sinners and saints—we all have an ongoing need for the Atonement of Jesus Christ to cleanse and heal us, yet we are saints despite our failings because we have been willing to take Jesus's name and enter into a covenant relationship with him. The Samaritan was not only an ethnic outsider, she was one whose choices might have made her seem ineligible as a servant of the Lord—but the Lord did not think so. As Latter-day Saint speaker Emily Belle Freeman has said, "The Lord will meet you where you are, as you are, but he doesn't intend to leave you there."[52] He will meet us, and if we accept him he will lift us as we receive and then share, the living waters that he brings.

NOTES

1. Bennema, *Encountering Jesus*, 161.
2. Morris, *The Gospel according to John*, 225.
3. Conway, *Men and Women in the Fourth Gospel*, 103–104.

4. See Julie A. Beck, "Mothers Who Know," *Ensign* (November 2007): 78, and chapter 2 above.
5. Shechem; Jerome and other early commentators equated Sychar with Shechem, (Brown, *Gospel according to John*, 169), though some modern commentators think that Sychar was a nearby village now known as Askar (Morris, *The Gospel according to John*, 227).
6. Siegfried H. Horn and P. Kyle McCarter, "The Divided Monarchy: The Kingdoms of Judah and Israel," *Ancient Israel: From Abraham to the Roman Destruction of the Temple*, ed. Hershel Shanks, third edition (Washington, DC: Biblical Archaeology Society, 2011), 132–35, 140, 163, 170–180.
7. Josephus, *Jewish Antiquities* 13.9.1 §255; *Jewish War* 1.2.6 §62 (Whiston, 438, 672). See the discussion of Jonathan Bourgel, "The Destruction of the Samaritan Temple by John Hyrcanus: A Reconsideration," *Journal of Biblical Literature* 135.3 (2016): 504, 511–513 and n. 65.
8. There is actual considerable evidence of intermarriage between the high priestly family of Jerusalem with the Samaritan governors of Samaria that suggests that the break between the two communities did not begin until the time of Alexander. See Frank M. Cross Jr., "Aspects of Samaritan and Jewish History in Late Persian and Hellenistic Times," *Harvard Theological Review* 59 (1966): 201–211.
9. Morris, *The Gospel according to John*, 226–27.
10. For more detailed discussions of the origins of the Samaritans and both their similarities and differences with the Judaism of Judea and the Galilee, see James D. Purvis, "The Samaritan Problem: A Case Study in Jewish Sectarianism in the Roman Era," *Traditions in Transformation: Turning Points in Biblical Faith*, ed. Baruch Halpern and John D. Levenson (Winona Lake, Indiana: Eisenbrauns, 1981) 232–250; Robert T. Anderson and Terry Giles, *The Keepers: An Introduction to the History and Culture of the Samaritans* (Peabody, Mass.: Hendrickson, 2002), 9–34, 17–134; and Stefan Schorch, "The Origin of the Samaritan Community," *Linguistic and Oriental Studies from Poznan* 7 (2005): 7–16.
11. Conway, *Men and Women in the Fourth Gospel*, 110–11.
12. For the rabbinic provision in Babylonian Talmud Šabbat 16b, see David Daube, "Jesus and the Samaritan Woman: The Meaning of *Synchraomai*," *Journal of Biblical Literature* 69.2 (1950): 137–38.
13. Turid Karlsen Seim, "Role of Women in the Gospel of John," *Aspects on the Johannine Literature*, ed. Lars Hartman and Birger Olsson (Stockholm: Almqvist & Wiksell International, 1987), 68.
14. Conway, *Men and Women in the Fourth Gospel*, 103; Bennema, *Encountering Jesus*, 162–63.

15. In addition to maintaining that the direct route through Samaria could be the fastest (*Life* 52 §269; Whiston, 33), Josephus also noted it was the one frequently used by Galileans, many of whom were more relaxed in their religious observance (see *Jewish Antiquities* 20.6.1 §118; Whiston, 649).
16. For the use of the Greek *dei* to indicate divine necessity, see Brown, *Gospel according to John*, 169; Morris, *The Gospel according to John*, 226; Conway, *Men and Women in the Fourth Gospel*, 105.
17. Conway, *Men and Women in the Fourth Gospel*, 104.
18. Adele Reinhartz, "A Feminist Commentary on the Gospel of John," *Searching the Scripture: A Feminist Introduction*, vol. 2, ed. by Elizabeth Schüssler Fiorenza (New York: Crossroad, 1994), 572–73, 599 n. 23.
19. Brown, *Gospel according to John*, 169; Conway, *Men and Women in the Fourth Gospel*, 106.
20. Morris, *The Gospel according to John*, 228.
21. Although the description "a Jew" can sometimes have a negative connotation in John, referring to the religious leadership or opposition to Jesus, in this context she is contrasting Jesus's ethnic background with hers. See Conway, *Men and Women in the Fourth Gospel*, 103 Mary L. Coloe, "The Woman of Samaria: Her Characterization, Narrative, and Theological Significance," *Characters and Characterization in the Gospel of John*, 188.
22. Daube, "Jesus and the Samaritan Woman," 138–140. See also Brown, *Gospel according to John*, and Morris, *The Gospel according to John*, 229.
23. Brown, "Water Imagery and the Power and Presence of God," 294.
24. Brown, *Gospel according to John*, 170.
25. Morris, *The Gospel according to John*, 230–31.
26. Brown, *Gospel according to John*, 169. Sherri Brown, "Water Imagery and the Power and Presence of God in the Gospel of John," *Theology Today* 72.3 (2015): 294–95, notes that by drawing Jesus's attention to Jacob, the woman may, in fact, have been asking Jesus what he thought of what their relationship was given their shared Israelite history and connection with Jacob.
27. While Bauer, "Zaō," *Greek-English Lexicon*, 426, lists "be full of vitality, be lively . . . of spring water in contrast with cistern water" in its fourth entry, the fifth entry defines it as "to be life productive" and "offer life" in its fifth entry.
28. Brown, *Gospel according to John*, 170.
29. Brown, *Gospel according to John*, 170–71; Coloe, "The Woman of Samaria," 189.
30. Eric D. Huntsman, "And the Word Was Made Flesh," 59.
31. Bennema, *Encountering Jesus*, 165.
32. Brown, *Gospel according to John*, 171.

33. Morris, *The Gospel according to John*, 228.
34. Conway, *Men and Women in the Fourth Gospel*, 117–18, 120.
35. Josephus *Jewish Antiquities* 9.14.3 §288 (Whiston, 332) tries to reconcile this by reducing the number of gods to five to match the number of nations. See Brown, *Gospel according to John*, 171; Morris, *The Gospel according to John*, 235.
36. Brown, "Water Imagery and the Power and Presence of God," 295.
37. Coloe, "The Woman of Samaria," 190–91.
38. Brown, *Gospel according to John*, 172; see also Morris, *The Gospel according to John*, 240.
39. Brown, *Gospel according to John*, 172.
40. Coloe, "The Woman of Samaria," 192; Seim, "Role of Women in the Gospel of John, 68.
41. Conway, *Men and Women in the Fourth Gospel*, 107.
42. Seim,"Role of Women in the Gospel of John," 59, notes that all antagonism about Samaritans had vanished by this point, but they are still bound by cultural expectations regarding gender relations.
43. Bennema, *Encountering Jesus*, 167, 169.
44. Seim,"Role of Women in the Gospel of John," 69.
45. Brown, *Gospel according to John*, 175.
46. Conway, *Men and Women in the Fourth Gospel*, 125.
47. Coloe, "The Woman of Samaria," 168.
48. Bennema, *Encountering Jesus*, 170–71.
49. Linda King Newell and Valeen Tippetts Avery, "Jane Manning James," *Ensign* (August 1979): 26–29; James Goldberg, "The Autobiography of Jane Manning James," Dec. 11, 2013, https://history.lds.org/article/jane-manning-james-life-sketch?lang=eng accessed 10 March 2018.
50. See Eric D. Huntsman, "Hard Sayings and Safe Spaces: Making Room for Struggle as Well As Faith," *Brigham Young University 2017–18 Speeches* (August 7, 2018), 4.
51. M. Russell Ballard, "The Trek Continues," *Ensign* (November 2017), 106.
52. Emily Belle Freeman, "Finding Grace Where You Are," lecture, Time Out for Women, 2018 tour.

CHAPTER 5

FOLLOWERS OF JESUS AND "HARD SAYINGS"

Murmur Not among Yourselves

> *"Then said Jesus unto the twelve, 'Will ye also go away?' Then Simon Peter answered him, 'Lord, to whom shall we go? thou hast the words of eternal life. And we believe and are sure that thou art that Christ, the Son of the living God.'" (John 6:68–69)*

When Jesus delivered his important and symbolic Bread of Life discourse (John 6:22–59) the reactions of the different groups of people who heard it provide examples of why people do and do not follow Jesus. Attracted by his healings and especially the miracle of the feeding of the five thousand, crowds had flocked to Jesus, eager for more bread and even desirous that he be made their king (John 6:2, 15). When Jesus eluded them by miraculously crossing the Sea of Galilee to Capernaum, the multitude followed him, largely because of the miraculous feeding, which was so reminiscent of how the Lord had fed their ancestors manna in the wilderness. While many members of the crowd failed to understand what Jesus meant when he said that he was "the bread come down from heaven," their leaders actively rejected him. Understanding that describing himself as "the bread come down from heaven" was a messianic claim, they reacted even more negatively to his declaration that they must symbolically eat his flesh and drink his blood (John 6:51–57). Indeed, even many of his own followers responded, "This is an hard saying; who can hear it?" and no longer followed him (John 6:60, 66).

The crowds had been initially enthusiastic about Jesus, but their interest waned when he started to teach and require something harder. This is often the case in the world today when many are not able to see Jesus as more than a great teacher. The Jewish leaders who opposed Jesus refused to consider his claims to be the "bread which came down from heaven" (John 6:41) and chose to be offended by his teachings. Likewise, some today are so rigidly committed to their own religious, political, scientific, or philosophic worldviews that they cannot entertain the restored truths about Jesus Christ and his gospel, especially when its claims are beyond what they are willing to accept. Yet it was those of Jesus's own disciples who chose to no longer walk with him who end up representing so many of us. Sometimes we might find it difficult to remain faithful when some challenging historical point, difficult principle, or uncomfortable policy becomes a "hard saying" that unsettles our discipleship. Perhaps even more disturbing and painful can be certain life challenges such as the loss of loved ones, opportunities, or dreams and other hard sayings such as gender disparities, sexual and other identities, and racial and ethnic discrimination. All of these might seem to call into question God's love for us or the love of our fellow saints.[1] This unsettling process only accelerates when we focus on what we do not understand or how others treat us, leading us to "murmur among ourselves," which often only intensifies our doubts or intensifies our pain (see John 6:43, 61).

The end of John 6, however, provides us the answer. When Jesus asked the Twelve if they would also leave him, Simon Peter responded by testifying, "Lord, to whom shall we go? thou hast the words of eternal life. And we believe and are sure that thou art that Christ, the Son of the living God" (John 6:68–69). Peter did not claim that Jesus's sayings had not been hard; rather he simply clung to the testimony of Christ that he did have. In this, he was like Nephi, who declared, "I know that he loveth his children; nevertheless, I do not know the meaning of all things" (1 Nephi 11:17). In the face of hard sayings that we do not understand or struggles that seem hard to bear, this is the testimony to which we, too, can hold fast, even when all else seems to fail.

MIRACULOUS SIGNS AND THE BREAD OF LIFE DISCOURSE

John 6:4 sets the Bread of Life discourse at Passover, a time that recalled the Lord's miraculous deliverance of his people from bondage, and the evangelist also connects it with two powerful miracles to underscore the discourse's connection with the exodus. In an act reminiscent of Moses's ascending Mount Sinai, Jesus went up a mountain in Galilee in a region that the synoptic Gospels identify as a wilderness (Greek, *erēmos topos*; KJV, "a desert place"). John further connects Jesus's teachings on the Bread of Life with the exodus experience by recounting two miraculous signs that echoed miracles that had blessed the children of Israel. These miracles are important for interpreting the discourse because rather than signifying powerful deeds as they do in the synoptic Gospels, miracles are in John first and foremost signs of who Jesus was. While in the synoptic Gospels miracles are usually described as "powerful deeds" (Greek, *dynameis*), John's miraculous signs (Greek *sēmeia*) were intended to reveal *who* Jesus was and *what* he came to do rather than just to demonstrate his power.[2] Because those who witnessed these miraculous signs failed to fully understand what they revealed about Jesus, they also failed to understand, or accept, what Jesus meant in his discourse.

The first miraculous sign before the Bread of Life discourse was the feeding of the five thousand (John 6:5–15), the only miracle attested in all four of the Gospels.[3] John's account of it provides details not found in the synoptic Gospels, noting, for instance, the roles played by Philip and Andrew, two of the first disciples to start following Jesus as described in John 1. Philip commented on the size of the crowd, wondering at the impossible expense of feeding them all. Andrew secured five loaves and two small fish, which Jesus then blessed and miraculously multiplied to feed the multitude that had followed him. Afterward, his disciples gathered twelve baskets of leftover food. This number, twelve, reflected the number of tribes that Moses had led into the wilderness and connected this miracle of provision with the manna by which Jehovah had sustained the children of Israel in the wilderness.[4]

When the crowd responded to this miracle by declaring, "This is of a truth that prophet that should come into the world" and tried to make him a king, Jesus withdrew to escape them (John 6:14–15). Because they saw the bread and what Jesus could do for them, the multitude saw him as a great past leader like Moses and perhaps as their hoped-for messianic king. Yet they failed to recognize that he was actually the same Jehovah who had given manna to their ancestors.[5] That evening, while Jesus remained alone on a mountain, his disciples, presumably the Twelve, set out across the Sea of Galilee toward Capernaum. The second miraculous sign before the discourse then occurred when a storm arose and threatened them, giving Jesus the opportunity to walk across the sea to their aid (John 6:16–21). Control of the elements was a power that the Old Testament attributed to Jehovah alone (see Job 9:8, 38:16; Habakkuk 3:15). When the disciples were frightened to see him walk across the water, Jesus underscored his divine identity by saying "*It is I*; be not afraid" (John 6:20, emphasis added). As with his "I Am" saying to the Samaritan woman in John 4:26, Jesus's use of the Greek phrase *egō eimi* here seems to have been a conscious claim that he was the very Jehovah who had revealed himself to Moses. Thus, just as Jehovah had parted the Red Sea for Moses and the Israelites to save them from the Egyptians, so Jesus strode on the sea of Galilee to save his friends from the storm. While they did not fully recognize his true identity at the time, this even clearer sign may have been what would later help the Twelve to respond with more faith to the Bread of Life discourse.

When the people followed Jesus to Capernaum the next day (John 6:22–25), Jesus delivered the discourse on the Bread of Life to them. Their different responses to the discourse reflect their varying understanding and levels of acceptance of Jesus. Commentators have generally interpreted Jesus's words about "eating his flesh and drinking his blood" (John 6:51–57) in two different ways, either sacramentally or metaphorically.[6] Because of our familiarity with the sacrament of the Lord's Supper from the synoptic Gospels, we readily see these passages as an anticipation of Jesus's saving suffering and death, which we now commemorate weekly with partaking of bread and water in the sacrament. At the time Jesus delivered this discourse, however, his audience would not have been familiar with this ordinance, and John's Gospel actually omits any mention of its institution when it later recounts the Last Supper (John 13:1–30). As a result, the response of Jesus's hearers would have varied depending upon the extent to which they understood and accepted his discourse metaphorically. In this sense, the imagery of eating and drinking the flesh and blood of Jesus would have first focused his listeners on how they needed to accept Jesus fully and internalize what he represented. Second, it presupposed that they would accept that Jesus—if he were the Messiah or Christ—actually needed to die, which was not a messianic expectation that even Jesus's disciples anticipated or were ready to accept at that time. Today we can use both interpretive approaches to understand better what we do each week when we partake of the sacrament. Taking it metaphorically stresses the necessity of accepting Jesus's death and making it part of us. Seeing its sacramental symbolism connects Jesus's statements about "eating his flesh and drinking his blood" with the bread and water used in the sacrament today. Regularly remembering Christ, accepting his saving death, and making it a true part of us can strengthen our ability to hold fast to the words of life even in times of a faith crisis.

CROWDS AND BREAD

Jesus delivered the first part of his Bread of Life discourse to a crowd that gathered along the shore at Capernaum. Having been miraculously fed the previous day (John 6:22–40), this group began to follow Jesus, perhaps expecting more (John 6:2, 22–25). As a group, the crowd is not as obvious a character as individuals in John have been, but the crowd in John 6 nevertheless acts as a character.[7] Its consistent identity as a group is underscored by the fact that although the King James sometimes refers to it as a multitude, a company, or a simply "the people" (John 6:2, 5, 22, 24), the Greek text uses the same word, *ho ochlos* meaning "a crowd," each time.[8] Because John often uses the verb "follow" to indicate discipleship, the crowd's following Jesus is a promising sign that they are potential disciples.[9] As is the case with other anonymous characters in John's Gospel, this nameless crowd is actually a character that we can identify with groups in our own day.

Jesus immediately told the crowd that he knew that they had come because of the previous day's miracle, suggesting that what they wanted for him was more miraculously-provided food. Moses had promised that a prophet would come "like unto him" (Deuteronomy 18:15); therefore, accepting Jesus to be this figure, they apparently expected him to keep giving them bread, even as manna had come every day throughout the forty years Moses had led the children of Israel in the wilderness. Noting that the manna under Moses had quickly decayed and observing that even the bread that he had miraculously provided the previous day had left them hungry the next, Jesus told them that rather than seek food (Greek, *brōsin*; KJV, "meat") that perished, they should instead seek for food that "endureth unto everlasting life" (John 6:26–27). The crowd seemed to recognize that in that instance Jesus was speaking metaphorically of spiritual food, because their next question was, "What shall we do that we might work the works of God?" (John 6:28). In other words, they understood that he had been speaking of the word of God, which prophets often compared to food that could be eaten (see Jeremiah 15:16; Ezekiel 2:8; 3:1; compare also to 2 Nephi 31:21, which encourages us to "feast upon the word of God"). Just as the Lord had given their ancestors manna in the wilderness through Moses, he had, even more importantly, given them his law. If this Jesus who had fed them was the prophet like unto Moses, then he, too, would give them God's law.[10] In this respect, the crowds that had followed Jesus to Capernaum seem to have viewed him as some do today—as a great teacher, a profound philosopher, and a singular moral example but perhaps no more than that.

Nevertheless, these would-be followers of Jesus were still concerned with getting their daily bread from him, as they seemed to insinuate when they reminded him, "Our fathers did eat manna in the desert; as it is written, He gave them bread from heaven to eat" (John 6:31). Jesus not only tried to shift the discussion back to God's word when he spoke of "true bread from heaven," he also tried to help them understand that he, in fact, was the Word of God himself (see John 1:1–3). Still, when he declared, "For the bread of God is he which cometh down from heaven, and giveth life unto the world" (John 6:33), his statement was more ambiguous than it seems to read in English. In Greek, "cometh down from heaven" (*ho katabainōn*) refers as easily to bread (Greek, *artos*) coming down from heaven as it might to an implied person (KJV, "he which cometh down"). As a result, when they enthusiastically cried, "Lord, evermore give us this bread," he needed to explicitly declare, "*I am the bread of life*: he that cometh to me shall never hunger; and he that believeth on me *shall never thirst*" (John 6:34–35, emphases added). This direct statement not only included another "I Am" statement implying that Jesus was Jehovah, its reference to "never thirsting" also reminds us of Jesus's teaching to the Samaritan woman (see John 4:13–14).[11]

There is no indication that the crowd understood, let alone accepted, what Jesus declared to them about himself. Instead, Jesus closes this part of his discourse by noting not only that they did not believe him but also that only those whom the Father had given him would come to him and have everlasting life (see John 6:36–40). They had seen the miraculous sign of the bread as a powerful deed rather than a sign. Then, failing to understand who Jesus was, they focused instead on the miracle itself—and what it did for them in a worldly sense—rather than on who Jesus was and what he had come to do for them in a spiritual and more eternal sense. Because the crowd had followed Jesus for the wrong reason and then continued to misunderstand him, those in the crowd did not continue to follow him.[12] Similarly, admiring, respecting, and even following the teachings of Jesus is not enough today if we do not fully accept and internalize that he is the Son of God come down from heaven to save us.

The Jewish Leaders and Symbolism

At this point in the narrative, the crowd with its inadequate faith faded from view, but another, more aggressive group came forward to oppose Jesus, one that John identified simply as "the Jews" (Greek, *hoi Ioudaioi*). Frequently, but not always, the Gospel of John uses the expression "the Jews" to refer to the religious opposition to Jesus. While it was used neutrally in the Nicodemus story in John 3 and to refer to Jesus himself in John 4, the term is used almost exclusively in the negative after the healing of the man at the Pool of Bethesda in John 5. From that point on it usually represents the religious leadership in Jerusalem and perhaps their supporters elsewhere throughout the land.[13] As a result, although Jesus, his disciples, and the members of the crowd were all Jewish, "the Jews" here in John 6 mostly likely represent either authorities from Jerusalem who had come to investigate Jesus's teaching or local Pharisees from Galilee. Such men would have been in a better position to understand the meaning behind the symbolism that Jesus used in his discourse,[14] yet if they did understand it, they chose to resist or be offended by it. Taking "the Jews" collectively as a character, we can see them as representing leaders of all types in our own society—religious, cultural, educational, and civic—who are often resistant to anything new, including the claims of the restored gospel.

There appears to be a change of venue for the second part of Jesus's discourse (John 6:41–59) from an outdoor location to the synagogue in Capernaum, which would not have been able to accommodate many more people than Jesus, his disciples, and those religious leaders who began to oppose Jesus more actively. As soon as these leaders are introduced, John notes that "The Jews then *murmured* at him, because he said, I am the bread which came down from heaven" (John 6:41, emphasis added). The murmuring of the Jewish leaders here is reminiscent of the repeated grumbling and complaining of the children of Israel against Moses, and it reminds readers of the constant murmuring of Laman and Lemuel against Nephi in the Book of Mormon. The Greek word for "murmured," *egongyzon,* used here in the imperfect tense, means that they began or kept muttering, grumbling, or complaining,[15] and their attitude kept them from even trying to understand the things that Jesus spoke to them. Unlike the crowds, the Jewish leaders understood that when Jesus said he had come down from heaven, he meant that he was a messianic, eschatological, or even divine figure. Indeed, they responded by asking, "Is not this Jesus, the son of Joseph, whose father and mother we know? how is it then that he saith, I came down from heaven?" (John 6:42). This was a clear refutation that Jesus might actually be the Son of God. Set in their minds as to their own religious views and expectations, the evangelist presented them as not being prepared—or willing—to even consider Jesus's claims.

Jesus's response was to drive home that not accepting him as the bread of life was cutting them off from eternal life, pointedly declaring, "Your fathers did eat manna in the wilderness, and are dead. This is the bread which cometh down from heaven, that a man may eat thereof, and not die" (John 6:49–50).[16] He then shifted to a more jarring image than the simple bread imagery that he had used with the crowds, declaring, "I am the living bread which came down from heaven: if any man eat of this bread, he shall live for ever: and *the bread that I will give is my flesh*, which I will give for the life of the world" (John 6:51, emphasis added). When his opponents complained, "How can this man give us his flesh to eat?" (John 6:52), their complaint seems disingenuous, because as religious leaders educated in religious discussions and imagery they should have understood that Jesus was speaking symbolically.[17]

Yet while Jesus had only asked the crowds to accept that he was the bread, or Word of God, come down from heaven, he demanded that "the Jews," and we, needed to eat his flesh and drink his blood in order to have eternal life and be raised up at the last day (see John 6:54). By using the language of eating and drinking, Jesus was metaphorically making at least two different points. First, eating and drinking means to incorporate—that is, to fully accept and make something a part of us. In other words, Jesus challenged both his original audience and us to receive him completely, accepting who he is and making him a part of ourselves: "He that eateth my flesh, and drinketh my blood, dwelleth in me, and I in him" (John

6:56). Second, in response to the Jews' earlier query, "How can this man give us his flesh to eat?" Jesus also signified that he would die so that all could live. In this scene, however, his opponents not only disputed his divine identity, they also rejected his saving work by choosing to recoil from the symbolism of eating his flesh and blood.[18] In the same way, unless people are willing to gain a testimony of Jesus's divinity and saving death today and then enter into a covenant with him, they deprive themselves of the eternal life that he offers.

Many Disciples Walked No More with Him

Unfortunately, these religious leaders were not the only ones who were offended by Jesus's teaching about accepting his salvific work: "Many therefore of his disciples, when they had heard this, said, This is an hard saying; who can hear it?" (John 6:60). The disciples here present another nameless, corporate character—this time one that consisted of those who had accepted Jesus as their Messiah, perhaps even as the Son of God, and had actively chosen to follow him. Yet while they accepted *who* he was, they had not yet come to a real understanding of *what* he had come to do. Contemporary messianic expectations had focused on a restorer and teacher like the one awaited by the Samaritans or a lawgiver and miracle worker like Moses such as the crowds had expected; and, increasingly, on an anointed king like David of old who would restore Israel. Though Psalm 22 and the later prophecies of Isaiah (e.g., 42:1–9; 49:1–7; 50:4–9; 52:13–53:12) had spoken of a suffering servant figure, few, including Jesus's own disciples, seemed to have had a clear conception of a messiah who would die as a sacrifice. In this regard, John wrote, "When Jesus knew in himself that his disciples *murmured* at it, he said unto them, Doth this *offend* you?" (John 6:61, emphases added).[19]

The fact that the same word for *murmur* was used for these offended disciples as had earlier been used for "the Jews" is significant.[20] The Jewish leaders had been secure, even unbending, in their own religious views and presuppositions. These disciples were similarly so firm in their previous messianic expectations and religious understanding that they were unable, or unwilling, to accept a new doctrine, even when it came from Jesus himself. Sometimes even we—particularly when serving as leaders or teachers or even just as faithful "members in the ranks"—can be so certain that we know how things are that we complain when new information, even new revelation, comes. And as was the case with the children of Israel or Nephi's brothers, complaining in groups builds upon itself, causing dissatisfaction to fester. Discontent, cynicism, or excessive doubt blocks inspiration and undermines belief. As Jesus taught his complaining disciples, "*It is the spirit that quickeneth*; the flesh profiteth nothing: the words that I speak unto you, *they are spirit*, and they are life. But there are some of you that believe not" (John 6:64–64, emphasis added). Because "quickeneth" means to make alive, here Jesus was explaining that only the spirit of God, which accompanied his words, could bring understanding to those who heard them.

While the word for *offend* (Greek, *skandalizō*) means to repel, shock, or give cause to anger, it originally meant to cause to fall or trip.[21] A hard saying usually starts as a stumbling block, something unexpected or confusing that causes us to stumble as we strive to follow Jesus. From there, however, it can grow into something that offends us or even causes us anger, which can lead us to leave the path of discipleship altogether. As John wrote, "From that time many of his disciples went back, and walked no more with him" (John 6:69). Sadly, our own age certainly has its own share of hard sayings. Elder Neal A. Maxwell (1926–2004), a member of the Twelve from 1981 until his death in 2004, wrote, "There are equivalent 'hard sayings' about our secular societies that one hesitates to utter but which need to be heard. They are not popular . . . A truth may touch us, bore us, or merely make us uncomfortable. But those are reactions to truth, and reactions do not alter the reality of truth itself."[22] Historical questions, former racial attitudes, the behavior of past and even current leaders, difficult doctrines, the roles of women, the sometimes unkind treatment of LGBTQ+ individuals by other members, and policies that impact social issues such as contemporary views of marriage equality or the status of the children of same sex couples can also be hard sayings for us that require additional faith to understand or at least accept in faith until better understanding comes through the inspiration of the Spirit or future revelation.[23]

HOLDING FAST TO THE WORDS OF LIFE

After the departure of many of his disciples, Jesus looked at the Twelve and asked, perhaps plaintively, "Will ye also go away?" (John 6:67). The reference to his inner circle of his twelve closest disciples is significant. As noted in the introduction, the Gospel of John's emphasis on discipleship more broadly leads it to focus less on the Twelve, who are only explicitly mentioned as a group twice here and then once in the upper room after Jesus's resurrection (John 6:67, 70; 20:24). Nevertheless, they are assumed to be present in most instances when Jesus's disciples are present, and at various places where John's Gospel identifies eight (perhaps nine if Nathanael is the same as the synoptic Barnabas) of the Twelve who are known from the apostolic lists in the other Gospels. Although frequently slow to understand Jesus and his teachings, they all nonetheless stay firmly by Jesus's side, with the exception of Judas Iscariot.[24] As a group, then, they can represent so many of us in the Church today who do not always understand everything about the gospel or why the Lord and his Church do what they do but nonetheless hold on in faith.

Simon Peter, who was one of the first disciples called and whose character is developed later in the Gospel, represents the group here when he replies to Jesus's question with one of his own: "Lord, to whom shall we go? thou hast *the words of eternal life*" (John 6:68, emphasis added). Not only does Peter's reference here echo Jesus's earlier teachings about eternal life that were woven throughout the Bread of Life discourse,[25] it also has resonance with the opening of the Gospel, which describes Jesus, the Divine Word, as the source of life and the one who came to give power to those who received him to become the sons and daughters of God (see John 1:4, 12). While there is no clear indication that Peter and the Twelve understood all of Jesus's teachings in the discourse much better than any of the others who heard it did, they apparently still believed them, recognizing the Spirit when Jesus spoke and trusting that his words brought life (John 6:63). Peter then testified, "And we believe and are sure that thou art that Christ, the Son of the living God" (6:69). This parallels the fullest version of Peter's confession at Caesarea Philippi, recorded in Matthew: "Thou art the Christ, the Son of the living God" (Mathew 16:16).[26] Although some of the earliest Greek manuscripts read a bit differently,[27] the effect is the same. While the Twelve would not fully understand Jesus's purpose until after his death and resurrection, their experiences with Jesus and the testimony of the Spirit so far had brought them to the point where they could still hold fast to the words of life despite uncertainty.

Just as such a testimony helped Peter and the Twelve press forward in their discipleship even in the face of a "hard saying," it can help all of us in the face of faith crises or life's challenges. In 2015, Patrick Mason, Howard W. Hunter Chair in Mormon Studies at Claremont Graduate University, published a study and reflection on how to deal with challenges of faith that he entitled *Planted:*

Belief and Belonging in an Age of Doubt. After reviewing some of the historical and doctrinal questions that trouble some members of the Church, he observed that "in too many of our stories we have treated the branches—historical figures and incidents and points of doctrine—in isolation from the Vine that give them life and constant nourishment."[28] In other words, when we are firmly planted in Jesus Christ, having a testimony of who he is and what he has done for us, we are better able to contextualize, understand, and, when we cannot understand, accept in faith issues that trouble us. Later, Mason continued, "A Christocentric worldview is not naïve towards the world's (and the church's) moral complexities, conundrums, and compromises—neither does it surrender to them, animated and anchored as it is by hope in Christ."[29]

As people whom I care for have struggled with faith issues in recent years, I have encouraged them—and myself—to fall back on the foundations of our testimonies and lived spiritual experience. And when any of our own faith flags, it is incumbent upon us to support and be patient with each other, listening and providing spaces of love, testimony, understanding, and acceptance as we seek to nurture or rekindle that faith.[30] For me it is the peace I find in Christ, the forgiveness I have found in repentance, and the closeness to God and power that I have felt in the ordinances of the priesthood, particularly the sacrament and the sacred ceremonies of the House of the Lord. Can we allow "hard sayings" of one type or another to force us to let these go? With Peter we should ask, "to whom shall we go?" While the discourse on the Bread of Life in its context is probably best understood metaphorically, there is also strength in a sacramental interpretation. When we partake of the emblems of Jesus's broken flesh and spilled blood, we do many powerful things in that single ordinance. By renewing our covenant to be willing to take his name upon us, always remember him, and keep his commandments, we are making Christ and his teachings a greater part of us. Yet the apostle Paul also taught, "For as often as ye eat this bread, and drink this cup, ye do *shew* the Lord's death till he come" (1 Corinthians 11:26, emphasis added). In Greek, "shew" actually means "proclaim," meaning that each time we take the sacrament we testify to ourselves, to our fellow saints, and to the Lord himself that we accept that Jesus truly suffered, died, and rose again for us. This testimony, strengthened each week through the sacrament of the Lord's Supper, thus becomes "an anchor of the soul, both sure and steadfast" (Hebrews 6:19; see also Ether 12:4).

Notes

1. See Huntsman, "Hard Sayings and Safe Spaces: Making Room for Struggle as Well As Faith," 1.
2. See Huntsman, *Miracles of Jesus*, 3, 135–36.
3. Mark 6:32–44; parallels Matthew 14:13–21; Luke 9:10–17. See the discussions of Huntsman, *Miracles of Jesus*, 29.
4. Morris, *Gospel according to John*, 301–302; Huntsman, *Miracles of Jesus*, 25–26, 29–30.
5. Eric D. Huntsman, "The Bread of Life Sermon" *Celebrating Easter*, edited by Thomas A. Wayment and Keith Wilson (Provo, UT: Religious Studies Center, 2006), 91–94.
6. Huntsman, "The Bread of Life Sermon," 88–89.
7. Bennema, *Encountering Jesus*, 201.
8. Huntsman, "The Bread of Life Sermon," 88, 92, 97.
9. Bennema, *Encountering Jesus*, 202.
10. Huntsman, "The Bread of Life Sermon," 94–95. Bertil Gärtner, *John 6 and the Jewish Passover*, Coniectanea Neotestamentica 17 (Copenhagen: Enjar Munksgaard, 1959), 41, and Morris, *Gospel according to John*, 319, both note that at this time manna or bread could be a symbol for the Torah.
11. Brown, *Gospel according to John*, 262–63; Morris, *Gospel according to John*, 322–23; Huntsman, "The Bread of Life Sermon," 95–96.
12. Bennema, *Encountering Jesus*, 222.
13. These religious and social elites were drawn primarily from those Jews who had returned from the Babylonian exile with a new focus on the Mosaic law and its requirements, as opposed to the common people who had remained in Judea and Galilee. This more religiously strict and educated group—from whom both the Pharisees and Sadducees mentioned in the New Testament emerged—had imposed themselves as leaders

throughout the land. For this and other arguments concerning the origins and composition of *hoi Ioudaioi* as presented in John, see David G. Burke, "Translating *hoi Ioudaioi* in the New Testament," *Explorations* (American Interfaith Institute) 9 (1995): 1–7; Daniel Boyarin, "The *Ioudaioi* in John and the Prehistory of 'Judaism,'" *Pauline Conversations in Context*, eds. Janice Capel Anderson, Philip Harl Sellew, and Claudia Setzer (Sheffield: Continuum, 2002), 216–240; Cornelis Bennema, "The Identity and Composition of OI IOYΔAIOI in the Gospel of John," *Tyndale Bulletin* 60.2 (2009): 239–263.

14. Bennema, *Encountering Jesus*, 91–92, 203. Along these lines Talmage, *Jesus the Christ*, 341, had written, "There were present in the synagogue some rulers—Pharisees, scribes, rabbis—and these, designated collectively as the Jews, criticized Jesus. . . . Chiefly to this class rather than to the promiscuous crowd who had hastened after him, Jesus appears to have addressed the remainder of his discourse."
15. Bauer, "gongyzō," *Greek-English Lexicon*, 204.
16. Huntsman, "The Bread of Life Sermon," 98–100.
17. Talmage, *Jesus the Christ*, 342, 347 n. 10.
18. Bennema, *Encountering Jesus*, 91.
19. Huntsman, "The Bread of Life Sermon," 103.
20. Conway, *Men and Women in the Fourth Gospel*, 166.
21. Bauer, "skandalizō" and "skandalon," *Greek-English Lexicon*, 926.
22. Neal A. Maxwell, *Wherefore, Ye Must Press Forward* (Salt Lake City: Deseret Book, 1977), 6–7.
23. Huntsman, "Hard Sayings and Safe Spaces," 1–2.
24. Bennema, *Encountering Jesus*, 225–26, refers to them as being "slow but sticky" because of their obtuse faithfulness.
25. Conway, *Men and Women in the Fourth Gospel*, 167.
26. Mark 8:29, the earliest Synoptic account of Peter's confession, reads simply "Thou art the Christ," and Luke 9:20 has "the Christ of God."
27. Some of the earliest and best Greek manuscripts of this passage read "We have believed, and have come to know, that you are the Holy One of God" (John 6:69 NRSV). See Metzger, *Textual Commentary*, 184, and the discussion of Brown, *Gospel according to John*, 298, 301–302. The phrase "Holy One of God" is not attested elsewhere in John, and it appears in the other gospels only in Mark 1:24 and Luke 4:34. Still, the rareness of the expression might be a mark of genuineness (Conway, *Men and Women in the Fourth Gospel*, 167–69).
28. Patrick Q. Mason, *Planted: Belief and Belonging in an Age of Doubt* (Provo, UT: Neal A. Maxwell Institute and Salt Lake City: Deseret Book, 2015), 119.
29. Mason, *Planted*, 123.

30. President M. Russell Ballard has written, "We need to listen to and understand what our LGBT brothers and sisters are feeling and experiencing. Certainly we must do better than we have done in the past *so that all members feel they have a spiritual home where their brothers and sisters love them* and where they have a place to worship and serve the Lord" (M. Russell Ballard, "Questions and Answers," *Brigham Young University 2017–18 Speeches* (August 14, 2017), 3, emphasis added. See also, Huntsman, "Hard Sayings and Safe Spaces," 4–7.

CHAPTER 6

FRIENDS OF JESUS

Lord, If Thou Hadst Been Here . . .

"Now Jesus loved Martha, and her sister, and Lazarus." (John 11:3)

Unlike the Twelve, whom the synoptic Gospels portray as giving up everything to follow Jesus full-time as disciples (see Mark 1:16–20; parallels Matthew 4:18–22; Luke 5:1–11), Martha, Lazarus, and Mary appear in John's Gospel as disciples who were devoted to Jesus but stayed in their own home and continued their own daily lives. These three siblings lived in Bethany, a village on the eastern slope of the Mount of Olives only two miles from Jerusalem, and their home there provided a convenient base for Jesus when he visited the holy city. Bethany, whose name means either "house of the poor" or "house of misery," may have been known for its almshouses or hospices that cared for the sick, poor, and dying outside of Jerusalem.[1] Still, the family seems to have been fairly prosperous, their home being large enough to entertain not only Jesus but also the Twelve and perhaps other disciples—such as Mary Magdalene, Joanna, Susanna, and the other women of Galilee who supported the ministry (see Luke 8:1–3)—who traveled with him. They were wealthy enough to own a private, rock-hewn family tomb, and Mary was able to afford the extravagantly expensive ointment that she used to anoint Jesus (John 12:3–5).[2] They were socially respectable enough that after

Lazarus's death he had among his mourners some of "the Jews," who in John seem to have represented the elite of Jerusalem, suggesting that the family members were accepted by the community despite their relationship with Jesus.[3] However, the most important thing we can draw from their experience is seeing them as friends of Jesus—John is explicit that Jesus loved Martha, Mary, and Lazarus, and two other times others comment on how much Jesus loved Lazarus (John 11:3, 5, 36).

Dorothy Lee's study of appearances of the siblings in both Luke and John suggests that their birth order was Martha, Lazarus, and Mary, with the two sisters representing some of the common, though sometimes stereotypical, traits of oldest and youngest children. Martha is responsible, even assertive, while Mary, though quiet, is intense and independent.[4] Lazarus, on the other hand, is a completely passive character—he never speaks in John and is always acted upon by others. Outside of John, these figures appear only in the Gospel of Luke, which was written before John but seems to have shared with it some common source material.[5] In Luke, the sisters are known from the story of Martha serving dinner while Mary sat listening at Jesus's feet (Luke 10:38–42), and Lazarus of Bethany may have been the inspiration for the parable of the poor beggar and the rich man (Luke 16:19–31).[6] In John, these three friends of Jesus are central to the longest sustained narrative in John, which is placed at a pivotal point at the conclusion of the first half of the Gospel, sometimes known as the Book of Signs (John 2:1–11:57), and the beginning of the second half, which is known as the Book of Glory (12:1–20:31).[7]

Because of the importance of the Bethany episodes in the Gospel, it is worth noting how the evangelist has structured them. The episodes involving the family form a chiasm, which places the raising of Lazarus from the dead at the important central point but also balances the interactions of the two sisters with Jesus:[8]

- Threat to Lazarus: his fatal sickness (11:1–16)
    - ***Martha and Jesus: her confession*** (11:17–27)
        - Belief of some of the "Jews" that came to Mary and the unbelief of others (11:28–37)
            - ***Raising of Lazarus*** (11:38–44)
        - Unbelief of some of the "Jews" that came to Mary and the belief of others (11:45–57)
    - ***Mary and Jesus: her act of anointing*** (12:1–8)
- Threat to Lazarus: leaders of "the Jews" plot against him (12:9–11)

The death of Lazarus was not caused by Jesus's delay in traveling to Bethany when he heard of Lazarus's illness, though both sisters believed that if Jesus, who was so well known for his healing miracles, had been there, Lazarus would not have died (John 11:21, 32). The message that they sent would have taken a day to get to where Jesus was on the other side of the Jordan, and even though he delayed two days before setting out to Bethany, it would have taken another day to get there. Because Lazarus had been dead four days when Jesus arrived, Lazarus must have died soon after his sisters sent the message. What his delay did provide was the opportunity for Martha and Mary to move from grief to greater understanding and deeper faith.[9]

From the outset of Lazarus's illness, Jesus had stated that it would be for the glory of both God and his Son (John 11:4). Because he did not immediately heal or raise Lazarus, the story establishes that God's glory does not always consist of sparing those whom he loves from the challenges of life or its loss.[10] Jesus's expressed love for the members of this family, and their clear devotion to him as Lord, makes the family ideal representatives of believers today. The members of this family were not "special witnesses," as were the Twelve, who followed Jesus full-time. Nevertheless, they had great faith, voiced fervent testimony, were the recipients of a powerful miracle, and expressed great love through practical and symbolic acts. The fact that their devotion to and friendship with the Lord is portrayed in the context of terrible loss and miraculous blessing makes them particularly powerful models for us as disciples today.

THE TESTIMONY OF MARTHA

In Luke, Martha is portrayed as a responsible hostess who was so distracted with serving (Greek, *perispaō*; KJV, "cumbered about")[11] that she failed to take advantage of the opportunity to sit at the feet of Jesus and learn from him as her sister Mary did (Luke 10:38–42). Jesus's double repetition of her name in that instance suggests more sympathy than judgment in his gentle correction,[12] and importantly he did not rebuke her for her service but only for her being overly anxious and upset by it (Greek, *merimnais kai torybazēi*; KJV, "careful and troubled").[13] John's portrayal of Martha lacks any negative description of her and develops her character further, showing her moving forward in her understanding and faith.[14] It is clear that while service was an integral part of her character (see John 12:1), Martha's response at the death of her brother shows that she had clearly taken advantage of opportunities to listen to, learn from, and develop trust in Jesus. In this, Martha represents believers who deal with death and loss in the light of their faith.[15]

Even in her grief, as soon as Martha heard that Jesus was approaching Bethany, she left her house and immediately went out to greet him (John 11:20). While she expressed the conviction that Jesus could have healed her brother and forestalled his death if he had been there, she immediately expressed confidence "that even now, whatsoever thou wilt ask of God, God will give it thee" (John 11:21–22). When Jesus assured her that her brother would rise again, Martha does not expect an immediate miracle. Rather, she understands Jesus's words as a reference to the final, future resurrection, perhaps taking them as the kind of consolation that might have been common in that day even as it often is among believers today.[16] Sensing her faith, Jesus turns the course of their conversation to his own role, declaring, "*I am* the resurrection, and the life: *he that believeth in me, though he were dead, yet shall he live*" (John 11:25, emphases added).

Jesus's declaration here begins with another "I AM" statement, one that connected himself with Jehovah, the God of Israel, and echoed his pronouncement to the Samaritan woman in John 5:28–29. Beyond that, it anticipated both the miracle he was about to perform in raising Lazarus from death as well as the glorious resurrection that his own coming conquest of death would make possible. Jesus's next declaration, however, presented another important truth that is sometimes overlooked: "And whosoever liveth and believeth in me shall never die. Believest thou this?" (John 11:26). Lazarus, like so many believers since, had believed in Jesus, yet he had died, suggesting that Jesus must have meant something besides physical death when he taught that they would never die. The belief in a literal, physical resurrection is a fundamental part of what biblical scholars call *future eschatology*. Eschatology is "the study of the end times," and in theology it is generally concerned with death and future events such as judgment, resurrection, and the final state of the soul. Frequently in John, as is the case here, Jesus teaches what is called *realized eschatology*. That is, believers can realize many of the final promised blessings of his Atonement here and now.[17] As a result, Jesus's teaching that those who believed in him would never die was more about how he had already overcome spiritual death for those who accept the spiritual life he offers. Understood in terms of realized eschatology, as believers we are alive in Christ and will never "die," or be separated from God, spiritually.[18]

We do not know how much of this Martha understood at that moment, but, like Peter after the Bread of Life discourse, she recognized the words of life when she heard them and responded with fervent testimony: "*Yea*, Lord: *I believe* that thou art the Christ, the Son of God, which should come into the world" (John 11:27, emphases added).[19] Her interjection, "Yea, Lord" (Greek, *nai kyrie*), is particularly emphatic in the original text, and her declaration, "I believe" (Greek, *pipesteuka*), is in the perfect tense, signifying, "I have come to believe and continue to believe now." Both of these elements show a firmness of conviction that echoes Peter's declaration "We believe and are sure," which was likewise in the perfect and can be rendered "We have believed and have come to know" (John 6:69 NAU).[20] In addition, Martha's confession contains elements of the testimonies of earlier disciples—Andrew, for instance, had recognized Jesus as the Messiah, or Christ, and Nathanael had proclaimed him as the Son of God.[21] Parallel with Peter's apostolic witness of Jesus, Martha's testimony points clearly to the purpose of the Gospel that its readers "might believe that Jesus is the Christ, the Son of God; and *that believing ye might have life through his name*" (John 20:31, emphasis added).[22]

In fact, Martha's is one of the only confessions in John that Jesus seems to have accepted as being complete and allowed to stand on its own. In other cases, he followed his followers' professions of belief with some degree of correction or further teaching, the only other clear exception being the declaration of the Samaritans that Jesus was "the Christ, the Saviour of the world" (John 4:42).[23] As soon as she finished testifying, Martha immediately went to get her sister, Mary, bringing her to Jesus. Leading others to Jesus, we have seen, is a fundamental component of discipleship in John. Just as Andrew went to get his brother Peter, Philip found Nathanael, and the Samaritan woman left her water jar to bring her townspeople to Jesus (John 1:40–42, 45; 4:28–29), so each of us is called to share our own testimony with others.

The Grief of Mary

When Mary heard from Martha that Jesus was coming, she immediately left the house and went to meet him. Perhaps without knowing it, in so doing she led some of "the Jews," who had come to mourn with her and Martha, to Jesus. These were neither rulers of the Jews in Jerusalem like Nicodemus nor local religious leaders such as those who had opposed Jesus at the Bread of Life discourse. Rather they seem to have been their supporters in the local aristocracy and established class from which Lazarus, Martha, and Mary themselves might have come.[24] When she left the house, they followed her, thinking that she was going to Lazarus's tomb to mourn for him there (John 11:31). Portrayed in this scene more positively than "the Jews" are elsewhere in the Gospel, they then witnessed both Jesus's interactions with Mary and his subsequent raising of Lazarus, which would lead some of them to begin to believe in him.

When Mary met Jesus, she fell on the ground before him and used the same words as Martha, declaring that he could have done something if he had been there. Although perhaps an implicit complaint, her words can also be taken as an indication of her earlier faith in Jesus as a healer.[25] Unlike Martha—who despite her grief was prepared to talk about the future resurrection and learn more about who Jesus was—Mary in that moment was overwhelmed with grief, dissolving into tears at Jesus's feet. In fact, John 11:33 describes Mary and the Jews who had followed her as not just crying but rather weeping loudly or even wailing (Greek, *klaiontas*).[26] Some commentators think that this display of uncontrolled grief bothered Jesus, leading to his being deeply moved (Greek *enebrimēsatō*; KJV, "groaned"), which can also be translated as angry, and troubled (Greek, *etaraxan*). Alternately, others suggest that he was disturbed at the power of Satan and the painful effects of the Fall and death, and others wonder whether he was frustrated by the lack of faith of those who had gathered to mourn Lazarus.[27]

While these are possible reasons, the fact that his deep feelings resulted in the shortest verse of scripture, "Jesus wept" (John 11:35), suggest another, more attractive motivation: compassion. Even though he knew that he would shortly raise Lazarus from the dead, his gentle weeping (Greek, *edakrysen* as opposed to Mary's *klaiousan*) modeled for us the responsibility that we all have as his followers to "mourn with those who mourn" (see Mosiah 18:9). His example shows us how well he understands and feels our pains and cautions us against minimizing the grief of others. While some who have suffered loss are more easily able to put it in a gospel perspective and are comforted by discussing the plan of salvation as Martha was, perhaps the best consolation we can offer those who grieve as Mary did is simply to express sorrow.[28]

The Raising of Lazarus

The name Lazarus (Hebrew, *La'zār*) literally means "God helps,"[29] and his rising from the dead constitutes the seventh and greatest miraculous sign in the Gospel of John.[30] While he is not a typical character—he is mute and completely passive in all the scenes in which he appears—Lazarus is still an important representative figure, standing for all who hear and obey Jesus's voice.[31] Further, as a disciple whom Jesus loved, he can be a representative of all Christians.[32] Another layer of symbolism is found in the fact that Jesus had put himself in some danger in order to come to Bethany to raise his friend; the Jewish leaders had recently sought his death because of his controversial teachings in Jerusalem, leading him to withdraw beyond the Jordan River (see John 10:31, 39–40; 11:7–8).[33] Yet, Jesus would later teach after the Last Supper, "Greater love hath no man than this, that a man lay down his life for his friends" (John 15:13). As a result, his willingness to endanger himself for

Lazarus was a foreshadowing of how he was actually willing to die for all of us because of his love for us.

When Jesus arrived at Lazarus's grave, he again expressed deep emotion before asking that the stone that covered the opening of the tomb be removed. This led Martha to express concern about the smell of decomposition that would be present given that Lazarus had been dead for four days (John 11:38–39). Because of a Jewish belief that the spirit of a dead person lingered near the body for three days,[34] this period of four days underscored that Lazarus was truly, irretrievably dead. As a result, contemporaries would have seen this as a greater miracle than the earlier raising of the son of the widow of Nain (Luke 7:11–17) or the daughter of Jairus (Mark 5:35–43; parallels Matthew 9:23–26; Luke 8:49–56), who were brought back to life shortly after their deaths. While Martha had expressed great faith in Jesus prior to arriving at the tomb, when he had spoken to her of Lazarus's rising, she may have been thinking of the final resurrection and might not have expected an immediate, miraculous resuscitation of her brother.[35]

When Jesus cried, "Lazarus, come forth" (John 11:43), his command echoed his earlier teaching on the resurrection from his discourse on the Divine Son, which had followed the healing of the man at the Pool of Bethesda in John 5. On that occasion, Jesus had taught, "For the hour is coming, in the which all that are in the graves shall hear his voice, And shall come forth; they that have done good, unto the resurrection of life; and they that have done evil, unto the resurrection of damnation" (John 5:28–29). Similarly, Jesus had taught that his sheep knew his voice (John 10:4). As a beloved disciple who knew Jesus, Lazarus immediately recognized Jesus's voice and obeyed, coming forth from the grave at his call. Lazarus' rising from the dead both anticipated and contrasted with Jesus's own coming resurrection. While both emerged from their tombs, Lazarus needed Jesus to call him forth, and he needed others to loose him from the grave clothes that bound him and remove the facecloth (Greek, *soudarion*; KJV, "napkin") that covered his face (John 11:44). Jesus, on the other hand, would come forth from the sepulcher on his own, leaving his grave clothes and facecloth behind (see John 10:18; 20:6–7). Although Jesus would rise with an immortal body, Lazarus was restored merely to mortal life. While Jesus left his grave clothes in the sepulcher, not needing them any longer, Lazarus brought his grave clothes with him, perhaps symbolizing that he would need them when he later died again.[36] Further, the presence of Lazarus's sisters at the tomb parallels the devoted women who would witness Jesus's own burial and resurrection.[37]

Though this miracle engendered faith in believers, it caused division among those who had come to mourn with Lazarus's sisters.[38] While many of "the Jews" who were present began to believe on Jesus, those who did not reported to the leading Pharisees in Jerusalem. This led to the convening of a meeting of the Sanhedrin that began to plot against Jesus, making the raising of Lazarus the proximate cause for his later arrest and death.[39] Likewise today, Jesus's ability to give both spiritual and actual life is often a cause of division, separating those who see him as merely a historical figure from those who accept him as the Christ, the Son of the living God.

The Supper in Bethany

After the chief priests and leading Pharisees met to conspire against Jesus (John 11:47–57), John records that the Bethany family hosted a special dinner for Jesus six days before Passover, perhaps in gratitude for the miracle that he had performed for them.[40] While Lazarus reclined (Greek, *anakeimenōn*; KJV, "sat") at the table with Jesus, Martha served the meal, recalling her efforts in the story recorded by Luke but without any sense of her being burdened by her efforts (John 12:1–2; see Luke 10:40–41). At this point, Mary anointed Jesus's feet with a pound of ointment, an extravagant amount, which Judas later complained was worth 300 days' wages (John 12:3, 5).[41] She further seemed to ignore social conventions by unbinding her hair and using it to wipe up the extra perfume (John 12:3).[42]

Mary's actions might have been motivated by her gratitude for what Jesus had done for her brother, but they also reflected the great love she had for him.[43] Love as a motivation connects this episode with the Last Supper as John records it. Indeed, Mary's act of wiping Jesus's feet uses the same word that John uses to describe how Jesus wiped and dried his disciples' feet (Greek, *ekmassō*) after the washing ceremony that he performed after the meal (John 13:5).[44] That act was a powerful expression of Jesus's love for his friends and his willingness to serve them, which he followed with the new commandment that they—and we—should love one another as he loved them (see John 13:24–35). Above all, however, Jesus stressed that Mary's act was prophetic—he explicitly claimed that she anointed him in preparation for his burial. In other words, while the male disciples had, to this point, failed to understand what Jesus's true mission was, Mary understood that he had come to Jerusalem to suffer and die (John 12:7–8).[45] Her symbolic action thus suggests revealed knowledge of both his identity and his salvific death.[46]

John's anointing scene closely parallels similar scenes in the other Gospels, including that of the woman who was a sinner earlier in the Galilean ministry (Luke 7:36–38) and the anointing by an unnamed woman that would take place midway through the Passion Week (Mark 4:3–9; parallel Matthew 26:6–13), raising the question of the relationship of the different incidents. The Lucan story shares with John's account of Mary's action the anointing of Jesus's feet, the wiping of them by a woman's hair, and the motivation of great love (see Luke 7:44–47). On the other hand, Luke's story occurred much earlier in Jesus's ministry and had no clear connection with Jesus's coming death. While Luke's account stands apart from the others, the stories in Mark, Matthew, and John share more features, in particular the emphasis on Mary, or the unnamed woman, acting to prepare Jesus for his burial. In addition to this explicit symbolism, Jesus's being anointed might implicitly symbolize how he was, in fact, Israel's rightfully anointed king and priest.[47]

On the other hand, the story that Mark and Matthew record states that the unnamed woman anointed Jesus's head rather than his feet, and the anointing takes place in the home of one Simon the Leper rather than in Martha's home. While it is impossible to determine whether John was simply presenting a different, and in many ways more detailed, version of the story in Mark and Matthew,[48] there are enough differences in detail to warrant taking them separately, and John's identification of Mary is especially significant because of her previous character development. For instance, her presence at Jesus's feet recalls her earlier falling at his feet in grief over the death of her brother. In both cases, being at his feet connotes worship, but it also reveals a progression in Mary's testimony; in addition to moving from grief to gratitude, she has moved from helplessness to action.[49] As Martha was earlier identified by her powerful confession, Mary is from this point remembered by her powerful act of love. Both women's acts remain models of how we as modern disciples can show our love for the Lord in both testimony and deed.

From Loss to Abundant Life in Christ

The stories of Jesus's friends at Bethany teach us much about the role of discipleship in responding to loss. Strengthened by her testimony, Martha not only provides a way of responding to grief with faith, she also presents herself as a model disciple, bearing a powerful, complete testimony of Jesus, bringing her sister to him, and then offering devoted service as she went on to serve him and her family.[50] Mary, on the other hand, represents the appropriateness of experiencing grief, showing that when we live together in love, we should "weep for the loss of them that die" (D&C 42:45). Mary found comfort not in words or doctrine but simply from being in the presence of her loving Savior, who mourned with her. She was quieter but also less conventional than her sister, yet in her own way Mary was still totally dedicated to Jesus, falling twice at his feet, devotion replacing grief.[51] Martha's faith was revealed in word, though still accompanied by service, while Mary's was in deed, in an action that was born from love and richly symbolic.[52] The narrative of John shows that the experiences and responses of both sisters were appropriate and acceptable. On the other hand, Lazarus, a character who does not speak and is acted upon rather than acting, represents how all of us are recipients of grace and saving power if we obey his call. Although Jesus's raising Lazarus from the dead prefigures our own certain future resurrection, as realized eschatology it also illustrates how each of us is spiritually dead until Jesus comes into our lives and calls us to new, spiritual life.

Many, if not most, of us have already experienced the wrenching loss of loved ones, be they parents, spouses, children, or dear friends. But the kind of grief that accompanies death also occurs with other kinds of loss, whether arising from disability, deep disappointment, chronic poor health, serious financial reverses, or from the lost faith or poor choices of loved ones. As beloved friends of Jesus Christ, we may find ourselves responding as Martha, Mary, or Lazarus did at different times. As heart-breaking as the death of my father and especially my mother was to me, perhaps the most difficult loss I have yet had to experience and accept was when our only son, Samuel, was diagnosed with autism when he was four years old. Though not unexpected, the official diagnosis was heartbreaking to me and my wife, Elaine; as so many of our hopes and dreams for our son were suddenly lost, it almost felt as if our young son had died. Still, as we have been strengthened by the Holy Ghost and the eternal perspective of the restored gospel, we have, like Martha, been able to accept his condition in faith and even see the blessings it has afforded us, Samuel, and so many others in our lives. In fact, I hardly teach, write, or speak without sharing the many miracles that we have witnessed as Samuel has often succeeded beyond all expectations and as he has developed into a young man of simple but genuine faith. Still, there are moments of heartbreak when he is hurt by others or frustrated with his disability, or when we mourn the life opportunities that we still fear he may not experience. In those moments, I feel like Mary, able to do nothing but fall on my knees and pour out my heart and grief to the Lord.[53]

One of those "Mary moments" occurred when Samuel was still quite small. In those days he would not go to sleep most nights without my putting him to bed, often reading over and over again his favorite story, *Green Eggs and Ham*. I remember one night when I had read that little book half a dozen times, I stopped, weary with the repetition and worried about what the future would hold for my boy. Would I be reading this same book over and over again sitting on the side of his bed in thirty or forty years? Bothered that I had stopped reading, Samuel tugged at me, beckoning me to read his favorite book yet again. As I gazed at my darling boy, I promised God I would do whatever Samuel needed as long as I lived. At that moment, the Lord called me from my deadly grief, opening to me a vision of Resurrection morning when a tall, handsome, and perfectly articulate man rose from his grave and threw his arms around me, thanking me for loving and taking care of him all those years. Filled with faith and hope, I felt like Lazarus at that moment, responding to the call and promise of the Spirit and able to walk forth with newness of hope.

In a latter-day revelation, the Lord promised that those who are true and faithful will receive a reward, "even peace in this world, and eternal life in the world to come" (D&C 59:23). When life is challenging and losses press on us, we often focus on the future, thinking of the joys of eternal life. I know that I certainly think of the blessing of the Resurrection, which will not only restore to us those whom we have lost but will also give us—and those whom we love—perfect, immortal bodies freed from all disability and flaws (see Alma 11:42–44). Jesus's miraculous raising of Lazarus certainly represented that, but it was his restoration to *this* life that gives me equal hope. In Jesus's discourse on the Good Shepherd, he proclaimed, "I am come that they might have life, and that they might have it more abundantly" (John 10:10). When we are alive in Christ, here and now, we have peace in this world and strength to not only endure its trials but have joy in the midst of them.

NOTES

1. Brown, *Gospel according to John*, 422; Brian J. Capper, "John, Qumran and Virtuoso Religion," *John, Qumran, and the Dead Sea Scrolls: Sixty Years of Discovery and Debate*, eds. Mary L. Coloe and Tom Thatcher (Atlanta, Georgia: Society of Biblical Literature, 2011), 93–116; Huntsman, *The Miracles of Jesus*, 114.
2. Bennema, *Encountering Jesus*, 267, 75–76; Huntsman, *The Miracles of Jesus*, 114.
3. Conway, *Men and Women in the Fourth Gospel*, 139; Huntsman, *The Miracles of Jesus*, 114.
4. Dorothy A. Lee, "Martha and Mary: Levels of Characterization in Luke and John," *Characters and Characterization in the Gospel of John*," 211–13.
5. Mark A. Matson, *In Dialogue with Another Gospel?* (Atlanta: Society of Biblical Literature, 2001), 153, 154–55.
6. J. F. Coakley, "The Anointing at Bethany and the Priority of John," *Journal of Biblical Literature* 107.2 (1988): 245–46
7. Brown, *Gospel according to John*, 429; Conway, *Men and Women in the Fourth Gospel*, 135.

8. See Lee, "Martha and Mary," 199–200; Gail O'Day, *The Word Disclosed: Preaching the Gospel of John*, revised and expanded (Atlanta: Chalice Press, 2002), 93–94.
9. Bennema, *Encountering Jesus*, 260, 278.
10. Morris, *Gospel according to John*, 478.
11. Bauer, "perispaō," *Greek-English Lexicon*, 804; G. Schneider, "perispaomai," *Exegetical Dictionary of the New Testament*, 3.76.
12. Lee, "Martha and Mary," 204.
13. Bauer, "merimnaō" and "thorybazō," *Greek-English Lexicon*, 458, 632. For a more detailed discussion of the tension between Luke's presentation of Martha and Mary in this passage, as well as an overview of different interpretive approaches to it, see Barbara A. Reid, *Choosing the Better Part: Women in the Gospel of Luke* (Collegeville, Minn.: The Liturgical Press, 1996), 144–58. For a Latter-day Saint reflection on the lessons of this story, see Bonnie D. Parkin, "Choosing Charity: That Good Part," *Ensign* (Nov. 2003): 104–106.
14. Lee, "Martha and Mary," 205.
15. Lee, "Martha and Mary," 208.
16. Morris, *Gospel according to John*, 488.
17. Brown, *Gospel according to John*, 425; Morris, *Gospel according to John*, 489.
18. Huntsman, *The Miracles of Jesus*, 115–16.
19. Brown, *Gospel according to John*, 425; Huntsman, *The Miracles of Jesus*, 116.
20. Conway, *Men and Women in the Fourth Gospel*, 141; Lee, "Martha and Mary," 203.
21. Conway, *Men and Women in the Fourth Gospe*l, 141–42.
22. In fact, some scholars, noting that some early manuscripts have Peter only say that Jesus was "the Holy One of God," maintain that Martha's testimony was the most complete and profound in John. See Bennema, *Encountering Jesus*, 262.
23. Conway, *Men and Women in the Fourth Gospel*, 143.
24. Brown, *Gospel according to John*, 427–28; Conway, *Men and Women in the Fourth Gospel*, 145; Bennema, "The Identity and Composition of OI IOYΔAIOI," 247–48.
25. Morris, *Gospel according to John*, 492.
26. Bauer, "klaiō," *Greek-English Lexicon*, 545; H. Balz, "klaiō," *Exegetical Dictionary of the New Testament*, 2.293–94.
27. Brown, *Gospel according to John*, 425–26; Morris, *Gospel according to John*, 493–96; O'Day, *The Word Disclosed*, 107–110; Bennema, *Encountering Jesus*, 268–69.

28. Huntsman, *The Miracles of Jesus*, 116–117, and "Hard Sayings and Safe Spaces," 2.
29. Brown, *Gospel according to John*, 422; Morris, *Gospel according to John*, 477 n. 12.
30. Huntsman, *The Miracles of Jesus*, 112.
31. Bennema, *Encountering Jesus*, 275.
32. Brown, *Gospel according to John*, 431.
33. Bennema, *Encountering Jesus*, 277.
34. Brown, *Gospel according to John*, 424; Morris, *Gospel according to John*, 485 and n. 40; Collins, "Representative Figures," 26.
35. Conway, *Men and Women in the Fourth Gospel*, 149.
36. Brown, Gospel according to John, 428; Collins, "Representative Figures," 46; Huntsman, *The Miracles of Jesus*, 117–18.
37. Conway, *Men and Women in the Fourth Gospel*, 139.
38. Morris, *Gospel according to John*, 499.
39. Brown, *Gospel according to John*, 428; Bennema, "The Identity and Composition of OI ΙΟΥΔΑΙΟΙ," 249–50.
40. O'Day, *The Word Disclosed*, 129.
41. Bennema, *Encountering Jesus*, 270.
42. While much is often made of the scandal of a woman uncovering, let along unbinding, her hair in public, Coakley, "The Anointing at Bethany," 250–52, correctly notes that this was a private gathering of family and friends. Still, the act of *wiping* Jesus's feet with her hair would have been unusual.
43. Coakley, "The Anointing at Bethany," 246.
44. O'Day, *The Word Disclosed*, 131.
45. Huntsman, *God So Loved the World*, 134–35; Julie M. Smith, "'She Hath Wrought a Good Work': The Anointing of Jesus in Mark's Gospel," *Studies in the Bible and Antiquity* 5 (2013): 32.
46. Lee, "Martha and Mary," 209.
47. Huntsman, *God So Loved the World*, 133–34; Smith, "She Hath Wrought a Great Work," 32–33.
48. Huntsman, *God So Loved the World*, 133; Smith, "She Hath Wrought a Great Work," 31–32. Morris, *Gospel according to John*, 506–510.
49. Lee, "Martha and Mary," 205–206.
50. Bennema, *Encountering Jesus*, 264–65.
51. Bennema, *Encountering Jesus*, 270.
52. Lee, "Martha and Mary," 209–210.
53. Huntsman, "Hard Sayings and Safe Spaces," 6–7.

CHAPTER 7

PETER AND THOMAS

Impulsive but Devoted Disciples

"Peter was grieved because he said unto him the third time, Lovest thou me? And he said unto him, Lord, thou knowest all things; thou knowest that I love thee. Jesus saith unto him, Feed my sheep." (John 21:17)

While Martha, Mary, and the Samaritan woman are relatively well-developed characters, the individual members of the Twelve receive less attention in the Gospel of John. Andrew and Philip, who are featured as two of the disciples first called in this Gospel, are only known to be members of the Twelve from the lists of apostles in the synoptic Gospels. Of the others from those lists, only Judas Iscariot and Thomas are ever explicitly described as being "of the Twelve" in John (see John 6:71; 20:24). In fact, this Gospel only presents Peter as one of the Twelve by implication when he speaks as their representative after the Bread of Life discourse (John 6:67–69). Of these three, Judas betrayed Jesus, and Peter and Thomas reveal themselves as devoted but at times either impulsive or hesitant followers.

Although John mentions Peter more than any other disciple,[1] he does not become a truly individual character until the last half of the Gospel.[2] Of those first called as disciples in John 1, Peter was the only one who, upon his introduction to Jesus, did not immediately make a Christological confession (John 1:41–42). When he did bear a strong testimony of Jesus after the Bread of Life discourse, he did so on behalf of all the Twelve (John 6:67–69). Beginning with the Last Supper scene in John 13, however, Peter's character becomes much more defined. While the nickname "the Rock" (Aramaic, *Kēphâ*; Greek, *Petros*) that Jesus gave him upon his first call reflected his character as it was later known,[3] he had to grow into the role of a steady, firm disciple. Instead, throughout the Gospel of John, Peter is often portrayed as outspoken and zealous for Jesus, but he also frequently misunderstood the Lord and was impulsive, overconfident, and even rash.[4] Yet his darkest moment, when he three times denied knowing Jesus or being one of his followers, stands out as Peter's greatest failing.

Thomas is only really known as a character in the Gospel of John; in the synoptic Gospels he only appears as a name in the apostolic lists (Mark 3:18; parallels Matthew 10:3; Luke 6:15). In three of his four appearances in John, he is called *Didymus*, Greek for "twin," which is the meaning of the Aramaic name *Thomas* (John 11:16; 20:24; 21:2).[5] He is first introduced at the beginning of the Lazarus story, where he bravely encouraged the other disciples to go with Jesus to Bethany "that we may die with him" (John 11:16). Still, his declaration on that occasion was fatalistic, expecting the worst, and he seems not to have taken seriously Jesus's foreknowledge that what was about to happen in Bethany was intended to build their faith (see John 11:15).[6] Although John also presents Thomas as an active participant in some of the discussion with Jesus after the Last Supper, Thomas is usually remembered as the one who did not believe the report of his fellow disciples that Jesus had risen from the dead.

Nevertheless, Peter and Thomas are both rehabilitated at the end of the Gospel, becoming important and powerful witnesses of Jesus's resurrection. Despite Peter's apparent failings in the hours leading up to Jesus's death and Thomas's hesitation following the

Lord's resurrection, we should be cautious about judging either of them too harshly. We must remember that John, even more than the other Gospels, frequently used historical figures as literary characters. Without freely manufacturing them, he used these people from Jesus's ministry to reflect particular types of disciples, which means that we often do not know much about the actual motivations and feelings of important figures such as Peter and Thomas.[7] As we have seen, the Gospel of John in particular uses its characters as types that represent different kinds of believers today. As a result, we can draw important lessons from the experiences—including the negative ones—of Peter and Thomas. First, those servants whom Jesus selects as his leaders are imperfect people with human weaknesses who sometimes make mistakes. We thus ought to extend to them the same charity that we ourselves expect and need.[8] Despite their lapses in faith and faithfulness, through Christ they overcame their weaknesses and went on to be powerful, faithful witnesses of him. Second, the contrast between their early failings and later, complete restorations is a powerful example of Christ's grace that can give us hope and encouragement. If the Lord was able to use such imperfect vessels, he will also forgive us and then use us in his kingdom as well.

Peter and Thomas at the Last Supper

One of the differences between John's presentation of the Last Supper and those found in the synoptic Gospels is that while the latter specifically mentioned the presence of the Twelve (Mark 14:17; parallels Matthew 26:20; Luke 22:14), John only speaks in broader terms of Jesus sharing this meal and its other activities "with his own" whom he had chosen out of the world (John 13:1, 18). Even in the synoptic Gospels, the explicit reference to the Twelve would not necessarily exclude the women who had followed

Jesus since Galilee and were later witnesses of the Crucifixion (see Mark 15:40–41). Indeed, a festal meal would also have naturally included these women and any of the disciples' families who were present. Yet even without this implication, because of John's consistently broader emphasis on all Jesus's disciples, it is easier for Christian readers of any age to imagine themselves as being part of the Savior's final night with his friends.[9] During John's narration of the evening's activities, Peter and, to a lesser extent, Thomas receive particular attention, and their behavior and questions can reflect the experiences that some of us as disciples also have.

Peter's first cameo occurs as John relates how Jesus washed his disciples' feet shortly after the conclusion of the meal. Having stripped off his outer garments, Jesus assumed the position of a servant, girding himself like a slave and moving around the outside of the table, washing the feet of his disciples (John 13:4–5).[10] The fact that Jesus intended this act to have symbolic, even ritual, significance is indicated by its timing; when the washing of feet was intended as a courtesy, it took place soon after a guest's arrival, not during or after the festivities had begun.[11] Because washing another's feet was a task generally reserved for slaves or women,[12] his act was clearly a symbol of humility and service, given Jesus's position as the master and teacher. In commemoration of this, many Christian denominations have preserved the tradition, practicing the washing of each other's feet during Easter week as a symbol of humility, mutual love, and service. For Latter-day Saints, this account evokes sacred ordinances, such as the ceremony accepting members of the school of the prophets (see D&C 88:138–141) and the initiatory ordinances of the temple. Biblical scholar Raymond Brown notes some possible deeper symbolism in Jesus's taking off (Greek, *tithēsin*) and then putting back on (Greek, *elaben*) his outer robe, acts which use the same words that are used for laying aside and taking back up his body before and after his death.[13] Accordingly, Jesus's act can be seen as foreshadowing the humiliation that he would soon suffer in his voluntary death on the cross, which would bring about the cleansing of those who come to him.[14]

When Jesus came to Peter and began to wash his feet, the strong-willed disciple initially refused, responding in a characteristically vigorous way (John 13:6–8a).[15] Explicitly, Peter objected to Jesus, his master, assuming the role of a servant to him. Peter's rejoinder, "Thou shalt *never* wash my feet" (Greek, *ou mē niphȩ̄s*), in fact, had the force of an oath or strong declaration.[16] If Jesus's stripping off his outer garments implicitly represented his coming death to save them, then Peter's attempt to stop him presents an interesting parallel with Peter's response to Jesus in the first passion prediction of Mark 8:31–33. In that passage, when Jesus prophesied that he would be betrayed, suffer, and die in Jerusalem, Peter rebuked him, being unwilling to even imagine that the man whom he had just testified was the Christ would die.[17] In John's account of the foot washing, Jesus also rebuked Peter, saying, "If I wash thee not, thou hast no part with me" (John 13:8b). Hearing this, Peter, in his usual fashion not wanting to do anything halfway, immediately insisted that Jesus wash his hands and feet as well,[18] leading Jesus to explain that the symbolic action was enough (John 13:9–10). Throughout the episode, Peter was intensely loyal and eager but showed a persistent lack of understanding.

After this, Jesus predicted his imminent betrayal, and Judas Iscariot left the company (John 13:21–30). To his remaining disciples, Jesus began to intimate that he would soon be leaving them, going to a place in a manner that they could not follow (John 13:33). After this he delivered his "new commandment" that they love one another as he had loved them (John 13:34–35). When Peter asked where Jesus was going, the Lord again replied that where he was going Peter could not follow, though later he would. With both his pride and his sense of devoted discipleship apparently hurt,[19] Peter declared, "Lord, why cannot I follow thee now? I will lay down my life for thy sake." (John 13:37). In response to

Peter's impulsive pledge, Jesus asked a pointed question and made a cutting prediction, saying, "Wilt thou lay down thy life for my sake? Verily, verily, I say unto thee, The cock shall not crow, till thou hast denied me thrice" (John 13:38). The fulfillment of this prediction would be the nadir of Peter's discipleship.

As a more minor character than Peter, Thomas receives less development in John. Still, he reveals a similar lack of understanding of Jesus and his mission. Thomas emerges from the group only briefly when Jesus turned from his prediction about Peter to address the general anxiety that his disciples were feeling considering his discussion of his imminent departure. After teaching them that he was going to prepare a place for them in his Father's house, Jesus told his disciples, "And whither I go ye know, and the way ye know" (John 14:4). In response, Thomas asked, "Lord, we know not whither thou goest; and how can we know the way?" (John 14:5). To this Jesus clearly declared, "I am the way, the truth, and the life: no man cometh unto the Father, but by me" (John 14:6). When Jesus said that he was "the way," it echoed his earlier declaration, "I am the door: by me if any man enter in, he shall be saved" (John 10:9), and it paralleled Book of Mormon teaching about "the strait and narrow path or way" (e.g., 1 Nephi 8:20; 2 Nephi 31:18–19; Jacob 6:11; 3 Nephi 14:4; 27:33; cf. Matthew 7:14). As one commentator has described, "Thomas appears in John as a loyal but dull disciple, whose misapprehensions serve to bring out the truth."[20] Although Thomas and the other disciples did not understand the full import of Jesus's declaration at the time, a few days later Thomas would gain a powerful witness in the form of Jesus's wounds and newly risen body. This could symbolize that we come to God only through his sacrificial death and glorious resurrection.

Because these reactions, these questions, and such confusion occurred at the Last Supper when Peter and Thomas were with Jesus, they can also have implications for us. Often we feel that if we are enjoying God's spirit or are in a setting where we are symbolically in his presence, then we should naturally behave better or be able to accept his will. Yet even when we feel close to the Lord, we may still fail to understand his plan for us or the meanings of some of his teachings. Although the ideal is to put off the natural man or woman through the Atonement of Christ, we are not always as "submissive, meek, humble, patient, full of love, willing to submit to all things which the Lord seeth fit to inflict upon him, even as a child doth submit to his father" as we would like to be (see Mosiah 3:19). When our old nature prevails or we make mistakes, we may still need to be humbled as Peter and Thomas were, but rather than reject us, the Lord continues to lovingly reach out to us.

The Denial of Peter

Because of our long tradition of respecting our leaders and trying to avoid unnecessary criticism, some Latter-day Saints have sought to excuse Peter or at least try to explain his behavior after Jesus's arrest. In 1971, Spencer W. Kimball (1895–1985), then acting president of the Twelve, said, "I do not pretend to know what Peter's mental reactions were nor what compelled him to say what he did that terrible night. But in light of his proven bravery, courage, great devotion, and limitless love for the Master, could we not give him the benefit of the doubt and at least forgive him as his Savior seems to have done so fully?"[21] Some have gone even further and tried to see implicit direction in Jesus's prediction that Peter would deny him three times that night, direction intended to preserve Peter so that he could lead the Church after Jesus's death. Such well-intentioned arguments, however, rely upon questionable grammatical arguments that do not even work in the case of the prediction as preserved in John 13:38.[22] Instead, the story of Peter and his denial in John, as in the other Gospels, fits an overall pattern that shows Jesus walking his atoning journey from Gethsemane to the cross totally alone—betrayed by Judas, abandoned by his disciples, falsely arrested and judged, abused, denied, and finally crucified as an innocent sacrifice for us.[23]

Peter's denial was anticipated by his impulsive and seemingly brave attempt to defend Jesus when a band sent by the chief priests came to arrest Jesus in Gethsemane. While all four Gospels note that one of Jesus's disciples resisted by cutting off the ear of a servant of the high priest (see Mark 14:47; parallels Matthew 26:51–52; Luke 22:50–51), only John's account identifies this bold disciple as Peter (John 18:10–11). In fact, John even identifies the name of the servant as Malchus, which becomes important later when Malchus's brother is one of those who witnesses one of Peter's denials (John 18:26). Despite Peter's loyal intentions, Jesus again rebuked him, saying, "Put up thy sword into the sheath: the cup which my Father hath given me, shall I not drink it?" (John 19:11). Not only was Peter inadvertently trying to keep Jesus from his destined saving death (again, see Mark 8:31–33), his actions here reveal that he did not fully understand the true nature of Jesus's kingdom or his mission. Later Jesus would explain to Pilate that his kingdom was not of this world—if it had been, his servants would have fought (John 18:36), suggesting that Peter's efforts at the arrest were not, in fact, those of one of his true servants.

Still, Peter's attempt to follow Jesus after his arrest (John 18:15) is a positive sign of discipleship, since "following" is a synonym for being a disciple, though his subsequent denials undercut his status as a loyal follower of Jesus.[24] After another disciple, very possibly the Beloved Disciple himself, arranged for Peter to be brought into the courtyard of the high priest, a servant girl who served as a doorkeeper immediately asked Peter whether he was one of Jesus's disciples (John 18:15–16). This elicited Peter's first denial, his declaration "I am not" (Greek, *ouk eimi*) contrasting with Jesus's previous I AM (*egō eimi*) affirmations.[25] Later, warming himself by a charcoal fire, Peter denied Jesus two more times, first to the crowd standing around the fire with him and then to Malchus's brother (John 18:25–27).[26] Significantly, Peter did not deny that Jesus was the Christ—in other words, he did not deny the sure testimony that in the synoptic Gospels he had received by revelation. Nevertheless, by denying that he knew Jesus or was one of his followers, Peter effectively recanted his discipleship.[27]

In this, Peter represents so many of us when we are not always true to our covenants, particularly our promise to take upon ourselves the name of Jesus Christ, always remember him, and keep his commandments. Though we do not usually deny our witness when we are disobedient or fail to be valiant in our testimonies of Jesus, nonetheless in those moments we belie our own pledges of loyalty to the Master. The poignant majesty of Jesus's Atonement is that in those moments—as in Peter's denials—Jesus nonetheless loved us and sacrificed for us. Peter's lack of loyalty—and frequently our own—was in a real way part of Jesus's lonely atoning journey. In a very real way, between Gethsemane and Golgotha Jesus not only suffered our sins, pains, and sorrows, he also experienced the terrible realities of betrayal, false judgment, arrest, and rejection. No wife betrayed by a husband, no child abused by a parent, no friend rejected by another person will fail to resonate with Jesus's being betrayed by the kiss of a friend, abandoned by his disciples, falsely accused and condemned and denied by Peter—and us.[28]

Doubting Thomas?

Despite Thomas's earlier, relatively positive portrayals, which depicted him as a faithful, believing disciple, his characterization abruptly changes with his reaction to the news of Jesus's resurrection. Jesus's appearance to ten of the Twelve on the evening of resurrection day (John 20:19–23) has a parallel with his appearance to all eleven of the remaining apostles in Luke 24:36–48. More than other resurrection appearances in these or the other Gospels, these two stress the literal, tangible nature of his resurrected body. In both scenes, Jesus appears, reveals the persistent signs of his crucifixion, and otherwise demonstrates that he has physically risen from the dead. The major difference, of course, is that in John's account, Thomas is not present when Jesus first appears. Thomas missed more than just witnessing the Risen Lord, however. In John, Jesus also commissioned his servants, endowed them with a special dispensation of the Holy Ghost, and gave them power to remit and retain sins (John 20:21–23). His unique bestowal of the Spirit upon them was richly symbolic: "he *breathed on them*, and saith unto them, Receive ye the Holy Ghost" (John 20:22, emphasis added).[29] Jesus's "breathing" the Spirit into them was evocative of the creation of Adam, when the Lord placed his spirit or "the breath of life" into the first man (Genesis 2:7).[30] It thereby signified a new creation, or rebirth through the Spirit, that Jesus had taught Nicodemus was necessary to enter the kingdom of God (see John 3:3–5).

By not being present at the first appearance, Thomas was deprived of both the apostolic commission and this transforming experience of the Spirit that his fellows had received.[31] Hearing from them that they had seen Jesus, Thomas insisted, "Except I shall see in his hands the print of the nails, and put my finger into the print of the nails, and thrust my hand into his side, *I will not believe*" (John 20:25, emphasis added). The Greek text uses a double negative construction (*ou mē pisteusō*) that indicates a strong denial.[32] Eight days later Jesus appeared to the assembled disciples, wishing them peace and bidding Thomas come forward to feel the wounds in his hands and the spearpoint's thrust in his side (John 20:27). His final command, "be not faithless, but believing," is more powerful in Greek than it is in the King James Version and can be rendered "do not persist in your unbelief but become a believer."[33] Thomas has thus traditionally been condemned on two points—first, for not believing his fellow disciples, and second, for demanding a marvelous additional sign.[34] Nevertheless, though John does not explicitly say that what Thomas had actually desired was the special witness of the tangible signs not only of Jesus's resurrection but also his atoning death, the fact that Jesus had offered these in the loose parallel found in Luke 24:39 may be significant. In Acts 1:3, that same author wrote of the apostles "whom also he shewed himself alive after his passion by *many infallible proofs*," where the Greek *pollois tekmēriois* can be translated as "by many sure signs or tokens."[35]

To his credit, Thomas believed and listened to Jesus as soon as he saw him, and Jesus's direction that Thomas feel his wounds showed that he knew what Thomas had said just a week before.[36] He immediately declared to Jesus, "My Lord, and my God" (John 20:28), which was the standard way that the Septuagint, or Greek translation of the Hebrew Bible, rendered *YHWH Elohāy*, or "the Lord my God."[37] In other words, Thomas declared that Jesus was Jehovah, the God of the Old Testament. This phrasing is also parallel to the opening proposition "and the Word was God" in the prologue of the Gospel (John 1:1), where "the Word" (Greek, *ho logos*) was the way of speaking of the premortal Christ.[38] Jesus's response to his confession was, "Thomas, because thou hast seen me, thou hast believed: blessed are they that have not seen, and yet have believed" (John 20:29). While this is often taken as a rebuke, it is a gentle one. After all, except for the Beloved Disciple, who believed upon seeing the grave clothes in the empty tomb (John 20:8), all others had also come to believe only when they saw the Risen Lord. Also, Jesus did not say that those who believe without seeing were *more* blessed than Thomas and others who had seen him were—simply that they, too, would be blessed.[39]

Given that most scholars believe that John 21, the epilogue of the Gospel, was an appendix added after the rest of John had already been composed, Thomas's confession would have been the last human statement in the original book. As a result, both

Thomas's sight-inspired belief *and* the testimony-inspired belief of subsequent Christians fulfill the purpose of the Gospel, which was that we all "might believe that Jesus is the Christ, the Son of God; and *that believing ye might have life through his name.*" (John 20:21, emphasis added). Indeed, a modern revelation teaches that different kinds of belief constitute different kinds of spiritual gifts: "To some it is given by the Holy Ghost *to know that Jesus Christ is the Son of God*, and that he was crucified for the sins of the world. To others it is given *to believe on their words*, that they also might have eternal life if they continue faithful" (D&C 42:13–14, emphases added). An important lesson from this may be that even amid our own doubts or periodic lack of belief, Jesus can still manifest himself to us. Significantly, such testimonies usually come in the company of other believers. In his meditation on "Doubting" Thomas, Patrick Mason observed, "In the moment of his greatest crisis, when he had absolutely no reason to believe and even less to stay, when it looked like everything he had lived and sacrificed for over the past three years was a complete sham, Thomas encountered Jesus, and he did so in communion with the [other] apostles."[40]

Peter's Threefold Affirmation of Love

The epilogue of the Gospel, consisting of its final chapter, features seven disciples who meet the Risen Lord by the Sea of Galilee. Among this chosen group are Thomas, Peter, and the figure of the Beloved Disciple himself.[41] Thomas's presence indicates that his confession at the end of the previous chapter qualified him to remain within the inner circle of Jesus's disciples. As a result, despite his earlier doubt or hesitation, he was about to be blessed with yet another post-resurrection witness. The central figure of this final scene, however, is Peter. Although he had been among the ten who had seen Jesus at the end of the first Easter day, he was not mentioned by name, which focuses his witness of Jesus's resurrection on this encounter. Significantly, although all four Gospels recount Peter's denial of Jesus, only John directly describes how the Lord rehabilitated and recommissioned him.[42]

Even in this final scene, traces of Peter's earlier tendency toward zeal and misunderstanding persist. When Jesus called to the seven, who had been fishing unsuccessfully, Peter did not recognize him (John 21:4). After the Lord's directions to the group resulted in a miraculous haul of fish, the Beloved Disciple recognized Jesus. Peter did not hesitate then. Quickly dressing, he impulsively threw himself into the water and swam to the shore ahead of the others to greet his Lord (John 21:8).[43] By then providing a meal for his disciples there on the shore (John 21:9–14), in a sense Jesus recreated the Last Supper, providing another setting where his friends could commune with him through table fellowship. At the conclusion of this meal, Jesus asked Peter three times whether Peter loved him. Each time when Peter affirmed that he did, Jesus enjoined him to feed his sheep or lambs (John 21:15–17). Although some commentators have tried to discern shades of meaning in the different Greek words that Jesus and Peter use for love in this passage, John actually uses these terms interchangeably in his Gospel.[44]

As a result, rather than seeing some pattern in the kind of love that Peter is capable of, the significance of Jesus's questioning of Peter is in the number of times that he asks Peter whether Peter loves him. Peter is pained at the third question because at that moment he seems to make the connection between Jesus's questioning of him and the number of times that he had denied Jesus.[45] Even the charcoal fire on which Jesus had cooked the fish that they ate that morning connects the scene with Peter's earlier denial, recalling the charcoal fire in the courtyard of the high priest (see John 18:18; 21:9).[46] Not only did Jesus give Peter a chance to compensate for each of the times that Peter had denied him, he follows each affirmation with a renewed charge for Peter to care for his flock. As Jesus is the Good Shepherd (John 10:11, 14), he recommissions Peter to serve as a "true undershepherd." As a shepherd-in-the-making, Peter serves as a symbol of all Christians-in-the-making—we can all be zealous for Jesus yet fail miserably or have a testimony of Jesus and still at times misunderstand him.[47] Peter's earlier stated willingness to lay his life down for Jesus was reminiscent of Jesus's repeated pledge to lay down his life for his sheep (see John 10:11; 13:37). In some of Jesus's final words to Peter, he prophesied that Peter would, in fact, one day suffer death for the Lord's sake (see John 21:18–19). Inasmuch as Peter represents all of us, even in our imperfections, we should ask ourselves what we are willing to give up for the Lord.

Faithful but Fallible Disciples

The mistakes and flaws of Peter and Thomas put them in a long string of noble but imperfect prophets. Their foibles or errors include the drunkenness of Noah, the situational untruthfulness of Abraham, the trickery and seeming deceit of Jacob, and Jonah's flight from his commission. While it is true that these faults appear in an imperfect record that reflected the cultural lenses and literary agendas of those who wrote and transmitted the scriptures, there is no reason why we should assume that great and otherwise good men—and women—never made mistakes. As is the case with all of us, their personal status was between them and the Lord, and we ought to assume that these faithful but fallible servants of the Lord repented and sought to make amends for any mistakes on their part. The fact remains that these figures of the past were justified by God, who still used them to accomplish great things. We should apply similar understanding and charity to leaders in our own dispensation. As Patrick Mason has encouraged, we should give the benefit of the doubt and be charitable to what others in our community's history might have said or done.[48]

If past and present prophets, apostles, and other leaders are likely to be faithful but at times fallible, how much more often are we, disciples-in-the-making, fallible but still faithful? To me the Lord's rehabilitation of Peter and his acceptance of the testimony of Thomas are signs of his great grace. If he could forgive them and then use them to accomplish great things in his kingdom, there is abundant hope for me and for you. Brent Top, a professor of Church history and doctrine and a former dean of Religious Education at Brigham Young University, has written, "I don't just empathize with Peter. I empathize with him because I see myself in him in many ways. I can relate to him. Like Peter, I have been known to impetuously do or say something that I regret within minutes. . . . [Peter] is my hero because of what he became—not what he made of himself, but what Christ made of him."[49] Likewise, we too find hope, strength, and opportunities to grow in grace in the body of Christ, composed of many devoted, if imperfect, members.

Notes

1. Bennema, *Encountering Jesus*, 111.
2. Conway, *Men and Women in the Fourth Gospel*, 169–170.
3. Bennema, *Encountering Jesus*, 111–12.
4. Conway, *Men and Women in the Fourth Gospel*, 170–73; Bennema, *Encountering Jesus*, 115–17, 123.
5. Brown, *Gospel according to John*, 424; Morris, *Gospel according to Thomas*, 483 n. 33. There is no way to know whether he was an actual twin, whether *Thomas/Didymus* was a proper name, or whether it was a nickname (Collins, "Who Are You?" 86–87).
6. Morris, *Gospel according to John*, 483–84.
7. Eric D. Huntsman, "The Accounts of Peter's Denial: Understanding the Texts and Motifs," *The Ministry of Peter, the Chief Apostle*, The 43rd Annual Sidney B. Sperry Symposium, eds. Frank F. Judd Jr., Eric D.

Huntsman, and Shon D. Hopkin (Provo, UT: Religious Studies Center; Salt Lake City: Deseret Book, 2014), 128–129.

8. Mason, *Planted*, 103–116.
9. Brown, *Gospel according to John*, 551 n. 5.
10. Morris, *Gospel according to John*, 547 n. 16, observes that the plural *himatia* suggests that Jesus removed *all* his clothes, leaving him in just a loincloth like a slave.
11. Morris, *Gospel according to John*, 544.
12. Brown, *Gospel according to John*, 564.
13. Brown, *Gospel according to John*, 551 n. 4.
14. Morris, *Gospel according to John*, 545, 547 n. 16.
15. Morris, *Gospel according to John*, 548.
16. Brown, *Gospel according to John*, 552 n. 8.
17. Brown, *Gospel according to John*, 566, 568.
18. Morris, *Gospel according to John*, 549.
19. Morris, *Gospel according to John*, 563.
20. Brown, *Gospel according to John*, 620 n. 6, quoting C. K. Barrett.
21. Spencer W. Kimball, "Peter, My Brother," *Speeches of the Year* (Provo, UT: Brigham Young University Press, 1971), 5.
22. See Huntsman, "The Accounts of Peter's Denial," 133–36. In short, arguments favoring a command from Jesus rather than a prediction suggest that the Gospels use a so-called imperatival future Greek verb for "thou shalt deny me thrice" (Mark 14:30; parallels Matthew 26:34; Luke 22:34). While this is a possibility for *aparnēsē* in Mark and Matthew, the similar-looking form in Luke and in John 13:28 is actually an aorist subjunctive in a completely different grammatical construction. All these questions, of course, revolve around what the evangelists who wrote the Gospels intended to convey, because Jesus himself would have been speaking in Aramaic and not Greek.
23. Huntsman, "The Accounts of Peter's Denial," 141.
24. Conway, *Men and Women in the Fourth Gospel*, 174.
25. Brown, *Gospel according to John*, 824.
26. Huntsman, "The Accounts of Peter's Denial," 139.
27. Bennema, *Encountering Jesus*, 118.
28. Huntsman, "The Accounts of Peter's Denial," 141.
29. Morris, *Gospel according to John*, 747–48.
30. Brown, *Gospel according to John*, 1022–23, 1037–39.
31. Collins, "Who Are You?" 88. The word "apostle" never appears in the King James Version of the Gospel of John, and the sole occurrence of the Greek *apostolos* appears in John 13:16, where it is translated as "The servant is not greater than his lord; neither *he that is sent* greater than he that sent him" (emphasis added). Nevertheless, in Jesus's post-resurrection

commission of the ten, he uses the verbal form *apestalken* when he says in John 20:21 that he was sending them "as my Father *hath sent* me" (emphasis added).

32. Brown, *Gospel according to John*, 1025 n. 25.
33. Brown, *Gospel according to John*, 1018–19, 1026.
34. Brown, *Gospel according to John*, 1045–46, notes that the earlier disciples had been content with just seeing Jesus's hands and side but Thomas wanted to actually feel them. However, just because John did not explicitly say that the ten felt the marks, this does not mean that they did not.
35. Bauer, "tekmērion," *Greek-English Lexicon*, 994.
36. Morris, *Gospel according to John*, 752–53.
37. Brown, *Gospel according to John*, 1047.
38. Brown, *Gospel according to John*, 1047–48; Morris, *Gospel according to John*, 753.
39. Morris, *Gospel according to John*, 753–54.
40. Mason, *Planted*, 132.
41. Morris, *Gospel according to John*, 760.
42. Conway, *Men and Women in the Fourth Gospel*, 176–77; Bennema, *Encountering Jesus*, 119.
43. Morris, *Gospel according to John*, 762–63.
44. Jesus uses *agapaō* in his first two questions and *phileō* in his third; Peter uses *phileō* in all three of his responses. While *agapaō* can refer to a higher love than the more friend-based meaning of *phileō* in some authors, such as Paul, this is not the case in John, who uses them interchangeably for variety (see Bauer, "agapaō" and "phileō," *Greek-English Lexicon*, 5–6, 1056–57; G. Schneider, "agapaō" and W. Feneberg, "*phileō*," *Exegetical Dictionary of the New Testament*, 1.8, 11–12; 3.425–26). For instance, *phileō* is used for the love of the Father for the Son (John 5:20) and for the Father for Jesus's disciples (16:27); conversely, *agapaō* is used for the love of people for darkness (3:19) and of "the Jews" for human approbation (12:43). See further Brown, *Gospel according to John*, 1102–03; Morris, *Gospel according to John*, 769–70; Bennema, *Encountering Jesus*, 120.
45. Brown, *Gospel according to John*, 1106; Morris, *Gospel according to John*, 767; Bennema, *Encountering Jesus*, 120–21.
46. Bennema, *Encountering Jesus*, 120–21.
47. Bennema, *Encountering Jesus*,124–25.
48. Mason, *Planted*, 77–81, 99–108.
49. Brent L. Top, "Fallible but Faithful: How Simon the Fisherman Became Peter the Rock," *The Ministry of Peter, the Chief Apostle*, The 43rd Annual Sidney B. Sperry Symposium, eds. Frank F. Judd Jr., Eric D. Huntsman, and Shon D. Hopkin (Provo: Religious Studies Center, and Salt Lake City: Deseret Book, 2014), 4, 11.

Conclusion

Becoming the Beloved Disciple

Fundamentals of Discipleship

"Then Peter, turning about, seeth the disciple whom Jesus loved following . . . Peter seeing him saith to Jesus, Lord, and what shall this man do?" (John 21:20–21)

The power of characterization in the Gospel of John has important application as we strive to live the restored gospel of Jesus Christ in the world today. Because the characters in John serve so well as types of the different responses people had to Jesus, those we have considered in this book can reflect the variety of ways people respond to the saving message of God's Son in our age. In this, I am struck by their diversity. Some disciples came to Jesus through the witness of others, while others found him independently. Some immediately recognized and followed him, while others, like Nicodemus, questioned more and took longer to come to their faith. In a time and culture that privileged men and a particular ancestral lineage, the experience of the Samaritan woman shows that in Christ there are no outsiders: all can come to him, find salvation, and share that joy with others. While some remained firm in their faith, challenges, even "hard sayings" from the Lord himself, could shake the convictions of others. Even leaders at times revealed themselves as imperfect disciples, but rather than focus on their mistakes, we should concentrate on how their master's dying and rising for them not only redeemed them, it also refashioned them as even stronger disciples. For those who were friends of Jesus—loving him and being loved by him—discipleship was stronger than grief, death, or loss.

Seeing this vast array of believers and their varied responses underscores that diversity in the family of Jesus Christ is real—and good. However, John's presentation of such a variety of experiences is not just a validation of diversity. This Gospel also contains a powerful call for unity. In his great Intercessory Prayer before his passion, Jesus pled, "Holy Father, keep through thine own name those whom thou hast given me, *that they may be one, as we are* . . . I in them, and thou in me, *that they may be made perfect in one*" (John 17:11, 23 emphases added). Despite our often differing walks with Jesus, what we should share is found in the Gospel of John's quintessential example of discipleship, the Beloved Disciple himself. Although his presence is suggested at different points within the Gospel, his explicit identification in four critical scenes emphasizes those fundamental characteristics of true discipleship that we should all share. These are the episodes where the disciple whom Jesus loved rested in the bosom of the Savior, where he stood at the foot of the cross, where he ran to the empty tomb, and finally, where he followed the Risen Lord, testifying that what he knew and had experienced was true.

Being Embraced by the Love of Jesus

After Jesus washed his disciples' feet at the Last Supper, he predicted his betrayal. As those present began to look at each other, wondering who would betray their master, the evangelist notes, "Now there was *leaning on Jesus's bosom* one of his disciples, *whom Jesus loved*." (John 13:23, emphases added). The reason for his position arose from the layout of the Last Supper itself. For festal occasions, such as Passover and other important meals, Jews in Jesus's time had adopted some of the banqueting practices of the Greeks and Romans, including an eating arrangement called the *triclinium*, which consisted of three couches arranged in a horseshoe. Dinner guests reclined on these couches on one elbow, usually their left, with their heads and hands oriented to a central low table while their feet pointed outward. Generally, they lay on these couches in pairs, with the guest of honor positioned in the middle of the central couch. With Jesus in this position, the Beloved Disciple would have been on the right-hand side of Jesus, with his head close to Jesus's chest.[1] The two were thus in close, intimate physical proximity to each other.[2]

While this was the literal meaning of the expression "leaning on Jesus's bosom" (Greek, *en tōi kolpōi*), the deeper symbolism can be found in the one other time that the expression is used in the Gospel. This is in the final verse of the *Logos* Hymn of the prologue, which describes the only begotten Son as being "in the bosom of the Father" (Greek, *eis ton kolpon*). The implication, then, is that the Beloved Disciple shared with Jesus the same kind of intimacy and love that the Son shares with the Father.[3] To the extent that the Beloved Disciple represents the position to which all of us as followers of Jesus aspire, beyond the historical aspect of this scene, it represents the love that we should and can share with the Lord. However we have come to know him, and whatever course our walk with him may have taken, like Lehi we can all declare, "I have beheld his glory, and I am encircled about eternally in the arms of his love" (2 Nephi 1:15).

To me the Last Supper setting provides an interpretive key to one of the important ways that we can find and experience this love. The Gospel of John makes no clear reference to the institution of the sacrament of the Lord's Supper, instead weaving its imagery and clues to its significance in other scenes, such as wine provided at the miracle at Cana and the declarations by Jesus in the Bread of Life discourse that we must "eat his flesh and drink his blood" to make him part of us and thereby allow us to attain eternal life (John 2:1–11; 6:51–59). Nevertheless, we know from the synoptic Gospels that Jesus established this sacred ordinance at the last meal that he shared with his disciples (see Mark 14:22–25; parallels Matthew 26:26–29; Luke 22:14–20). As a result, to me the image of John reclining in the bosom of Jesus at the Last Supper provides an image of our lying in the arms of his love as we partake of the sacrament. Beyond that, as we gather as the body of Christ to share the emblems of his body and blood, we commune not only with the Lord but with one another, gathering around his table as did his disciples of old. Indeed, all ordinances are "conduits of grace," or divinely established channels, by which the saving, strengthening, and transforming power of God comes into our lives.[4] As we participate in them, we receive, and share, his love.

Standing at the Foot of the Cross

The Beloved Disciple may well have been the "other disciple" who, with Peter, followed Jesus after he was arrested in Gethsemane (John 18:15–16), the word "followed" (Greek, *ēkolouthei*) being the Gospel of John's standard way of describing discipleship. The next scene in which the evangelist expressly identifies the disciple, however, is at the foot of the cross at Golgotha: "When Jesus therefore saw his mother, and *the disciple* standing by, *whom he loved*, he saith unto his mother, Woman, behold thy son!" (John 19:26, emphases added). As we have seen, the mother of Jesus was one of her son's foremost witnesses, knowing better than any other mortal that he was, in fact, God's own Son. Standing at the foot of the cross with the Lord's mother as she watched him die for the sins of the world, the Beloved Disciple joined her as an eyewitness of Jesus's redeeming death.[5] Inasmuch as the Beloved Disciple represents all of us as beloved disciples, in that moment he symbolizes each of us as we come to a personal knowledge that Jesus died for us.

When Jesus said, "Woman, behold thy son" to his mother, he followed this declaration by saying to the disciple whom he loved, "Behold thy mother!" and from that moment the disciple "took her unto his own home" (John 19:27). The standard understanding of this episode sees this as Jesus providing for his mother's care, but on a symbolic level, it can represent much more.[6] In particular, we can focus not so much on what this language of adoption did for Mary as on the change of status that it effected on the disciple. Whereas he had previously been a student or servant, when Mary became his mother, he was brought directly into the family of Christ,[7] just as we are when we are baptized and take his name upon ourselves. Although employing different family relationships, the speech of King Benjamin in the Book of Mormon similarly describes how the atoning sacrifice of Jesus Christ brings us into his family: "And now, because of the covenant which ye have made ye shall be called the children of Christ, his sons, and his daughters; for behold, this day he hath spiritually begotten you; for ye say that your hearts are changed through faith on his name; therefore, ye are born of him and have become his sons and his daughters" (Mosiah 5:7).

The Beloved Disciple filled one other role at the cross, that of a witness. When Jesus died, "one of the soldiers with a spear pierced his side, and forthwith came there out blood and water. And *he that saw it bare record, and his record is true*: and he knoweth that he saith true, that ye might believe" (John 19:34–35, emphasis added). Augustus M. Toplady (1740–1778) powerfully set this image with the words of his hymn, "Rock of Ages" when he penned the lines:

> Rock of Ages, cleft for me,
> Let me hide myself in thee;
> Let the water and the blood,
> From thy wounded side which flowed,

> Be of sin the double cure,
> Save from wrath and make me pure.[8]

But the stream of blood and water represented more than just what Jesus had *done*; it also symbolized who he *was*. It picked up the imagery that we saw at the wedding at Cana, where blood represented mortality and water symbolized divinity and eternal life.[9] As the son of Mary, Jesus was a man who could die as sacrifice for sin. As the Son of God, he was the divine Christ, who could work an infinite and eternal sacrifice (see Alma 34:8–10) with power to lay down his life and take it up again (see John 10:17–18).

Running to the Empty Tomb

When Mary Magdalene found the stone rolled away from the mouth of the sepulcher that first Easter morning, "she runneth, and cometh to Simon Peter, and to *the other disciple, whom Jesus loved*" (John 20:2). Wanting to know for themselves what had happened to the body of their Lord, the two ran to the tomb. The image of the two running as fast as they could, including the delightful detail that the other disciple outran Peter, creates a moving template for us. If the Beloved Disciple also represents all Christians, this scene poses a question for us. Does the mere possibility of the Resurrection fill us with such hope that we would eagerly run to find out for ourselves?

Another detail of this scene has implications for believers today. When the other disciple arrived, he waited and allowed Peter to enter the sepulchre first, where Peter "seeth the linen clothes lie, And the napkin, that was about his head, not lying with the linen clothes, but wrapped together in a place by itself" (John 20:6–7). When the other disciple went in afterward, "he saw, *and believed* (John 20:8, emphasis added). While there are different arguments about what the disposition of these grave clothes meant,[10] there seems to be an implicit contrast between the two characters. Peter went in and saw, while the Beloved Disciple went in, saw, and believed.[11] Whereas Mary Magdalene was the first one to see the actual Risen Lord, the Beloved Disciple was nonetheless the first to believe based upon the witness of the empty tomb and the sign of the discarded grave clothes. In this, he can represent believers throughout the ages who have hope in the Resurrection not because they have seen Jesus but because of faith.

We Know Our Testimony Is True

The Beloved Disciple was among the seven who met the Risen Lord by the Sea of Galilee. When Jesus called to them from the shore, he was the one who first recognized him: "Therefore that disciple whom Jesus loved saith unto Peter, It is the Lord." (John 21:7). Later, after Jesus prophesied to Peter of his own death as a martyr, "Peter, turning about, seeth the disciple whom Jesus loved *following*; which also leaned on his breast at supper . . ." (John 21:20, emphasis added). His unique title, the one whom Jesus loved, together with the reference to his intimacy at the Last Supper, are combined with the image of him following (Greek, *akolythounta*), once again the typical term in John indicating discipleship.[12] When Peter asked what would happen to the disciple, Jesus responded enigmatically, "If I will that he tarry till I come, what is that to thee?" (John 21:22–23). This declaration led to debate, ancient and modern, as to whether the Beloved Disciple would ever die.[13]

For Latter-day Saints, Doctrine and Covenants 7, which with other restoration scripture identifies the disciple as the apostle John, has largely resolved the question of the fate of the disciple, attesting that he was translated and will stay on the earth as a witness until Jesus comes again. As a type who potentially represents all disciples, however, the Beloved Disciple's presence here can also stress how believers in every age—regardless of whether they are alive when Jesus returns—must continue to follow Jesus. Even as the Lord directed Peter not to be concerned with the particular mission of the Beloved Disciple, so we, too, should not concern ourselves over the nature of the discipleship or the missions of others. What is important is that each of us keeps following Jesus Christ, trusting that our lives are in his hands.

One of the final two verses of the Gospel of John, which were, in all likelihood, added by a later editor,[14] attests to the truthfulness of the witness of the Beloved Disciple that stands at the heart of the entire book: "This is the disciple which testifieth of these things, and wrote these things: *and we know that his testimony is true*" (John 21:24, emphasis added). To the extent that we can, one last time, allow this figure to represent us, this verse should leave us reflecting on our own testimonies. Whatever our own discipleship looks like, however we came to the Lord, whatever faith issues we have wrestled with, whatever losses we have suffered, and whatever mistakes we have made, there are fundamentals that we should all share. As Peter asked, so we can ask: What shall we do? With the Beloved Disciple we can be embraced in the love of Jesus, which love we can feel and receive in great measure through priesthood ordinances. With him we can stand at the foot of the cross, firm in our faith in his atoning sacrifice. And with him we can run to the empty tomb, sustained by the hope that because he lives, we all shall live.

NOTES

1. Brown, *Gospel according to John*, 573–74; Morris, *Gospel according to John*, 555–56.
2. The disciple's position is stressed again when he is described in 13:25 as "lying on Jesus's breast" (Greek, *anapesōn . . . epi tou stēthos Iēsou*).

3. Brown, *Gospel according to John*, 577; Conway, *Men and Women in the Fourth Gospel*, 180–81; Beck, "Whom Jesus Loved," 225; Bennema, *Encountering Jesus*, 300.
4. Huntsman, *Worship*, 34–36, 40–44, 46, 48–54.
5. Beck, "Whom Jesus Loved," 228.
6. Earlier interpretations, for instance, included seeing Mary as representing Jewish Christianity, which was taken in by Gentile Christianity, or as the Church, with the disciple representing its membership that should care for and protect her (see Beck, "Whom Jesus Loved," 228).
7. Brown, *Gospel according to John*, 922–27; Conway, *Men and Women in the Fourth Gospel*, 184; Beck, "Whom Jesus Loved," 227–28.
8. Augustus M. Toplady, "Rock of Ages" *Sacred Songs No. 2*, eds. I. D. Sankey, J. McGranahan, G. Stebbins (New York: Biglow & Main Co., 1899), no. 99.
9. Brown, *Gospel according to John*, 946–52; Huntsman, "Word Made Flesh," 63–65.
10. Some commentators point out that grave robbers would not have bothered to remove them, so their presence suggested that Jesus had risen. Others, focusing on the particular placement of clothes, argue that they were left in the position in which they had been when Jesus was still wrapped in them, suggesting that his body had passed through them. See Brown, *Gospel according to John*, 1007–08; Morris, *Gospel according to John*, 735. I would suggest that upon rising Jesus would have first removed the facecloth (Greek, *soudarion*; KJV, "napkin"). Then, standing, he would have removed the linen cloths separately.
11. Beck, "Whom Jesus Loved," 229–30.
12. Beck, "Whom Jesus Loved," 231.
13. Jesus's prophecy can be taken either way, either to mean that the disciple would not die or simply as a statement by Jesus that his fate was not Peter's business. For the most part, biblical scholarship has either taken the latter, agnostic position or suggested that by the time the final edition of the Gospel was produced the Beloved Disciple, the source and guarantor of the witness behind the Gospel, had actually died, causing some consternation among the early Johannine Community. See, for example, Brown, *Gospel according to John*, 1110; Conway, *Men and Women in the Fourth Gospel*, 185.
14. Brown, *Gospel of John*, 1124, 1126–27; Morris, *Gospel of John*, 775–77.

APPENDIX A

THE *LOGOS* HYMN

Because the first section of the Gospel of John (1:1–18) consists of a poetic presentation of the premortal Christ as the Word of God, it is often called the *Logos* Hymn, because *logos* is the Greek term for "word" as well as for a wide semantic range of related concepts. The poetic stanzas about "the Word" are interspersed with descriptions of the prophet John in prose.[1]

Echoing the opening of the creation story when God brought forth first light and then all of creation by speaking (see Genesis 1:3–2:3), John describes Jesus as the Word, representing God's will, plan, and intent as well as the means by which he communicates and interacts with his creation. Because this hymn portrays the Word as divine and preexistent, it establishes the "high Christology" of the Gospel of John. Christology is the study of the person and work of Jesus—that is, what it means that he was the anointed servant of God and how he came to suffer and die to redeem the world. Of the four Gospels, John consistently portrays Jesus as the most divine, making it "higher" than the Christology of Mark, Matthew, and Luke.

1 In the beginning was the Word,
  and the Word was with God,
  and the Word was God.
2 The same was in the beginning with God.

3All things were made by him;
and without him was not any thing made that was made.
4In him was life;
and the life was the light of men.
5And the light shineth in darkness;
and the darkness comprehended it not.

6There was a man sent from God, whose name was John. 7The
same came for a witness, to bear witness of the Light, that all
men through him might believe. 8He was not that Light, but
was sent to bear witness of that Light.

9That was the true Light,
which lighteth every man that cometh into the world.
10He was in the world,
and the world was made by him,
and the world knew him not.
11He came unto his own,
and his own received him not.
12But as many as received him,
to them gave he power to become the sons of God,
even to them that believe on his name:
13Which were born, not of blood,
nor of the will of the flesh,
nor of the will of man,
but of God.
14And the Word was made flesh,
and dwelt among us,
(and we beheld his glory,
the glory as of the only begotten of the Father,)
full of grace and truth.

15John bare witness of him, and cried, saying, "This was he of
whom I spake, He that cometh after me is preferred before me:
for he was before me."

16And of his fulness have all we received,
and grace for grace.
17For the law was given by Moses,
but grace and truth came by Jesus Christ.

18No man hath seen God at any time;
the only begotten Son,
which is in the bosom of the Father,
he hath declared him.

NOTE

1. See Huntsman, "The Gospel according to John," in *New Testament History, Culture, and Society.*

Appendix B

Outline of the Gospel of John

The Gospel is divided into four major parts: a prologue (John 1:1–51); a major division focusing on the ministry of Jesus (2:1–11:57); another division focusing on Jesus's final week, culminating in his passion and resurrection (12:1–20:31); and an epilogue (21:1–25). The major section after the prologue is often called the "Book of Signs" because of the seven miraculous signs (Greek, *sēmeia*) found in it, though it also contains seven important dialogues or discourses. The next major division is often called "The Book of Glory" because John frequently describes the saving death and resurrection of Jesus as the means by which he is both glorified and glorifies the Father.

Characters discussed in this book appear in ***bold italics***.

- Prologue (John 1:1–51)
    - The *Logos* Hymn (John 1:1–18)
    - The First Witnesses and Disciples (1:19–51): ***The Prophet John, Andrew, the other disciple, Peter, Philip, and Nathanael***

- Book of Signs (John 2:1–11:54)
    - First Signs and Dialogues (John 2:1–4:54)
        - First Sign: Water to Wine at the Wedding at Cana (2:1–11): ***The Mother of Jesus***
        - Jesus at the First Passover, including the cleansing of the temple (2:13–25)
        - Dialogue with ***Nicodemus*** on the New Birth (3:1–15)
        - *Intervening material (3:16–36)*
        - Dialogue with ***the Samaritan Woman*** at the Well (4:4–26) and the response of the Samaritan village (4:27–45)
        - Second Sign: Healing the Nobleman's Son in Cana (4:46–54)
    - Signs and Discourses in the Context of Jewish Feasts (John 5:1–10:42)
        - Jesus on the Sabbath (*Shabbat*, 5:1–47)
            - Third Sign: Healing of the Lame Man at the Pool of Bethesda (5:1–16)
            - Discourse on the Divine Son (5:17–47)
        - Jesus at Passover (*Pesach*, 6:1–71)
            - Fourth Sign: Feeding of the 5,000 (6:5–15)
            - Fifth Sign: Walking on Water (6:16–21)
            - Discourse on the Bread of Life (6:26–59)
                - Words to ***the crowd*** (6:26–40)
                - Words to ***"the Jews"*** (6:41–59)
                - Words to and Reaction of ***His Disciples*** (6:60–71)
        - Jesus at Tabernacles (*Sukkot*, 7:1–10:21, commemorating Law, Water, and Light)
            - Discourse on the Life-Giving Spirit (7:16–44)
            - *Intervening material (7:45–53)*
            - [Story of the Adulteress (8:1–11)][1]

            - » Discourse on the Light of the World (8:12–59)
            - » Physical and Spiritual Blindness (9:1–41)
                - › Sixth Sign: Healing of the Man Born Blind (9:1–12) and the reaction to it (9:13–41)
            - » Discourse on the Good Shepherd (10:1–21)
        - ◆ Jesus at Dedication (*Chanukah*, 10:22–42)
    - o The Raising of Lazarus in Bethany (John 11:1–54)
        - ◆ Threat to Lazarus: his fatal sickness (11:1–16): ***Thomas***
        - ◆ ***Martha*** and Jesus: Jesus is the Resurrection and the Life and her confession (11:17–27)
        - ◆ Jesus mourns with ***Mary***: belief of some of the "Jews" that came to Mary and the unbelief of others (11:28–37)
        - ◆ Seventh Sign: Jesus Raises ***Lazarus*** from the Dead (11:38–46)
        - ◆ Unbelief of some of the "Jews" that came to Mary and the belief of others; the plot to kill Jesus (11:45–57)

- Book of Glory (John 12:1–20:31)
    - o Setting the Scene for the Passion (John 11:55–12:50)
        - ◆ ***Mary*** and Jesus: her act of anointing (12:1–8)
        - ◆ Threat to Lazarus: leaders of "the Jews" plot against him (12:9–11)
        - ◆ Jesus's Triumphal Entry (12:12–19)
        - ◆ *Intervening material (12:20–50)*
    - o The Last Supper and Its Activities (13:1–30)
        - ◆ The Theme of Love Introduced (13:1–2)
        - ◆ The Foot Washing and Its Lessons (13:3–20): ***Peter***
        - ◆ Jesus Foretells His Betrayal (13:21–30): ***The Beloved Disciple***

        - The New Commandment to Love One Another (13:31–35)
        - ***Peter***'s Denial Foretold (13:36–38)
    - The Farewell Discourses (John 14:1–16:33): ***Thomas***
    - The Great Intercessory Prayer (17:1–26)
    - The Passion of Jesus (John 18:1–19:42)
        - The Arrest of Jesus (18:1–11)
        - Jewish Hearing and Roman Trial (18:12–19:17a): ***Peter***
        - The Crucifixion and Burial (19:17b–42): ***The Mother of Jesus, Mary Magdalene, and the Beloved Disciple***
    - Resurrection (20:1–29)
        - The Empty Tomb (20:1–10): ***Mary Magdalene, Peter and the Beloved Disciple***
        - Jesus Appears to ***Mary Magdalene*** (20:11–18)
        - Jesus Appears to the Ten (20:19–23)
        - Jesus Appears to the Eleven, including ***Thomas*** (20:24–29)
    - The Purpose of the Gospel (20:30–31)

- Epilogue (John 21:1–25)
    - Jesus Appears to Seven at the Sea of Galilee (21:1–15)
    - Jesus and ***Simon Peter*** (21:15–19)
    - The Fate and Testimony of ***the Beloved Disciple*** (21:20–25)

NOTE

1. This pericope is ancient but generally held to be textually suspect, not appearing in the earliest and best Greek manuscripts of John (see Metzger, *Textual Commentary*, 187–89). Nevertheless, this passage may well preserve a genuine tradition about Jesus and fits the Sukkot context because of its connection with the Law.

Bibliography

Anderson, Robert T. and Terry Giles. *The Keepers: An Introduction to the History and Culture of the Samaritans.* Peabody, Mass.: Hendrickson, 2002.

Avery, Linda King Newell and Valeen Tippetts. "Jane Manning James." *Ensign*, August 1979: 26–29.

Ballard, M. Russell. "Questions and Answers." Pages 1–6 in *Brigham Young University 2017–18 Speeches.* Provo, Utah: Brigham Young University Publications and Graphics, August 14, 2017.

—. "The Trek Continues. " *Ensign*, November 2017: 104–106.

Balz, Horst and Gerhard Schneider, eds. *Exegetical Dictionary of the New Testament.* 3 vols. Grand Rapids, Mich.: Eerdmans, 1990–93.

Barney, Kevin L. "The Joseph Smith Translation and Ancient Texts of the Bible." *Dialogue: A Journal of Mormon Thought* 19, no. 3 (Fall 1986): 85–102.

Bauckham, Richard. *Gospel of Glory: Major Themes in Johannine Theology.* Grand Rapids, Mich.: Baker Academic, 2015.

—. *Jesus and the Eyewitnesses: The Gospels as Eyewitness Testimony.* Grand Rapids, Mich.: Eerdmans, 2006.

—. *The Testimony of the Beloved Disciple.* Grand Rapids, Mich.: Baker Academic, 2007.

Bauer, Walter. *A Greek English Lexicon of the New Testament and Other Early Christian Literature.* 3rd edition. Edited by Frederick William Danker. Translated by F. Wilbur Gingrich, and F. W. Danker William F. Arndt. Chicago: University of Chicago, 2000.

Beck, David R. "The Narrative Function of Anonymity in Fourth Gospel Characterization." *Semeia* 63 (1993): 143–158.

—. "'Whom Jesus Loved': Anonymity and Identity, Belief and Witness in the Fourth Gospel." Pages 221–239 in *Characters and Characterization in the Gospel of John*. Library of New Testament Studies 461. Edited by Christopher R. Skinner. New York: Bloomsbury, 2013.

Beck, Julie B. "Mothers Who Know." *Ensign*, November 2007: 76–78.

Bednar, David A. "A Reservoir of Living Water." Pages 1–10 in *Brigham Young University 2006–2007 Speeches*. Provo, Utah: Brigham Young University Publications and Graphics, 2006–2007.

Bennema, Cornelis. *Encountering Jesus: Characters in the Gospel of John*. Minneapolis: Fortress Press, 2014.

—. "The Identity and Composition of ΟΙ ΙΟΥΔΑΙΟΙ in the Gospel of John." *Tyndale Bulletin* 60, no. 2 (2009): 239–263.

Blomberg, Craig L. *The Historical Reliability of John's Gospel: Issues and Commentary*. Downer's Grove, Ill.: InterVarsity Press, 2001.

Bourgel, Jonathan. "The Destruction of the Samaritan Temple by John Hyrcanus: A Reconsideration." *Journal of Biblical Literature* 135, no. 3 (2016): 499–517.

Boyarin, Daniel. "The Ioudaioi in John and the Prehistory of 'Judaism'." Pages 216–39 in *Pauline Conversations in Context: Essays in Honor of Calvin J. Roetzel*. Edited by Philip Harl Sellew, and Claudia Setzer Janice Capel Anderson. Sheffield: Continuum, 2002.

Bradbury, Wm. B., ed. *Bradbury's Golden Shower of S.S. Melodies: A New Collection of Hymns and Tunes for the Sabbath School*. New York: Ivison, Phinney & Co., 1862.

Brown, Raymond E. *An Introduction to New Testament Christology.* New York: Paulist Press, 1994.

—. *An Introduction to the Gospel of John.* Edited by Francis J. Moloney. New York: Doubleday, 2003.

—. *An Introduction to the New Testament.* New Haven: Yale University Press, 1997.

—. *The Birth of the Messiah.* New Haven: Yale University Press, 1977; repr. 1993.

—. *The Gospel according to John.* Anchor Bible. Vols. 29 and 29A. New York: Doubleday, 1966.

Brown, Francis, S.R. Driver, and Charles A. Briggs. *The Brown-Drivers-Briggs Hebrew and English Lexicon.* Peabody, Mass.: Hendrickson, 2008.

Brown, S. Kent. *The Testimony of Luke.* Brigham Young University New Testament Commentary. Provo, Utah: BYU Studies, 2015.

Brown, Sherri. "Water Imagery and the Power and Presence of God in the Gospel of John." *Theology Today* 72, no. 3 (2015): 289–98.

Buckwalter, H. Douglas. *The Character and Purpose of Luke's Christology.* Cambridge: University Press, 1996.

Burke, David G. "Translating *Hoi Ioudaioi* in the New Testament." *Explorations (American Interfaith Institute)* 9 (1995): 1–7.

Byrne, Brendan. "The Faith of the Beloved Disciple and the Community in John 20." *Journal for the Study of the New Testament* 23 (1985): 83–97.

Capper, Brian J. "John, Qumran, and Virtuoso Religion." Pages 93–116 in *John, Qumran, and the Dead Sea Scrolls: Sixty Years of Discovery and Debate.* Edited by Mary L. Coloe and Tom Thatcher. Atlanta: Society of Biblical Literature, 2011.

Claybaugh, John D. "What the Latter-day Scriptures Teach about John the Beloved." Pages 16–35 in *The Testimony of John the Beloved.* Salt Lake City: Deseret Book, 1998.

Coakley, J. F. "The Anointing at Bethany and the Priority of John." *Journal of Biblical Literature*, 1988: 241–56.

Collins, Raymond F. "From John to the Beloved Disciples: An Essay on Johannine Characters." *Interpretation* 49 (1995): 359–69.

—. "Representative Figures." Pages 1–45 in *These Things Have Been Written: Studies on the Fourth Gospel*. Louvain Theological & Pastoral Monographs 2. Grand Rapids, Mich.: Eerdmans, 1990.

—. "'Who Are You?' Comparison/Contrast and Fourth Gospel Characterization." Pages 79–95 in *Characters and Characterization in the Gospel of John*. Edited by Christopher W. Skinner. Library of New Testament Studies 461. New York: Bloomsbury, 2013.

Coloe, Mary L. "The Woman of Samaria: Her Characterization, Narrative, and Theological Significance." Pages 182–96 in *Characters and Characterization in the Gospel of John*. Edited by Christopher W. Skinner. Library of New Testament Studies 461. New York: Bloomsbury, 2013.

Conway, Colleen M. *Men and Women in the Fourth Gospel: Gender and Johannine Characterization*. Atlanta: Society of Biblical Literature, 1999.

Cross, Frank M. Jr. "Aspects of Samaritan and Jewish History in Late Persian and Hellenistic Times." *Harvard Theological Review* 59 (1966): 201–211.

Crossan, John Dominic and Marcus Borg. *The First Christmas: What the Gospels Really Tell Us about Jesus' Birth*. New York: HarperOne, 2006.

Cullmann, Oscar. *The Christology of the New Testament*. Revised edition. Translated by Shirley C. Guthrie and Charles A. M. Hall. Philadelphia: Westminster Press, 1963.

Culpepper, R. Alan. *Anatomy of the Fourth Gospel*. Philadelphia: Fortress Press, 1983.

—. *John, The Son of Zebedee: The Life of a Legend.* Minneapolis: Fortress Press, 2000.

Edwards, Ruth B. *Discovering John: Content, Interpretation, Reception.* Grand Rapids, Mich.: Eerdmans, 2015.

Encyclopedia Judaica. "Witness," https://www.jewishvirtuallibrary.org/witness, accessed September 26, 2018.

Evans, Craig A. *Fabricating Jesus: How Modern Scholars Distort the Gospels.* Downers Grove, Ill.: IVP Books, 2006.

Gardner, Jane F. *Women in Roman Law and Society.* Bloomington and Indianapolis: Indiana University Press, 1986.

Givens, Terryl and Fiona. *The Crucible of Doubt: Reflections on the Quest for Faith.* Salt Lake City: Deseret Book, 2014.

Green, Joel B., Scot McKnight, and I. Howard Marshall. *Dictionary of Jesus and the Gospels.* Dower's Grove, Ill.: InterVarsity Press, 1992.

Hengel, Martin. *The Johannine Question.* Translated by John Bowden. Philadelphia: Trinity Press International, 1989.

Hillmer, Melvyn R. "They Believed in Him: Discipleship in the Johannine Tradition." Pages 77–97 in *Patterns of Discipleship in the New Testament.* Grand Rapids, Mich.: Eerdmans, 1996.

Holland, Jeffrey R. "Come and See." *The New Era*, December 1997: 4–8.

Holzapfel, Richard Neitzel. *A Lively Hope: The Suffering, Death, Resurrection, and Exaltation of Jesus Christ.* Salt Lake City: Bookcraft, 1999.

Holzapfel, Richard Neitzel, Eric D. Huntsman, and Thomas A. Wayment. *Jesus Christ and the World of the New Testament.* Salt Lake City: Deseret Book, 2006.

Horn, Siegfried H. and P. Kyle McCarter. "The Divided Monarchy: The Kingdoms of Judah and Israel." Pages 129–207 in *Ancient Israel: From Abraham to the Roman Destruction of the Temple.* Third Edition. Edited by Hershel Shanks. Washington, D.C.: Biblical Archaeology Society, 2011.

Huntsman, Eric D. "And the Word Was Made Flesh": A Latter-day Saint Exegesis of the Blood and Water Imagery in the Gospel of John." *Studies in the Bible and Antiquity*, 2009: 51–65.

—. *God So Loved the World: The Final Days of the Savior's Life.* Salt Lake City: Deseret Book, 2011.

—. *Good Tidings of Great Joy.* Salt Lake City: Deseret Book, 2011.

—. "The Gospel according to John." In *New Testament History, Culture, and Society.* Edited by Lincoln Blumell. Springville, Utah: Cedar Fort, 2018 forthcoming.

—. "Hard Sayings and Safe Spaces: Making Room for Struggle as Well As Faith." Pages 1–9 in *Brigham Young University 2017–18 Speeches.* Provo, Utah: Brigham Young University Publications and Graphics, August 7, 2018.

—. "Teaching through Exegesis: Helping Students Ask Questions of the Text." *Religious Educator* 6, no. 1 (2005): 107–126.

—. "The Accounts of Peter's Denial: Understanding the Texts and Motifs." Pages 127–149 in *The Ministry of Peter, the Chief Apostle: The 43rd Annual Sidney B. Sperry Symposium.* Edited by Eric D. Huntsman, and Shon D. Hopkin Frank F. Judd Jr. Provo and Salt Lake City: Religious Studies Center and Deseret Book, 2014.

—. "The Bread of Life Sermon." Pages 87–111 in *Celebrating Easter.* Edited by Thomas A. Wayment and Keith J. Wilson, Provo, UT: Religious Studies Center, 2006.

—. "The Lamb of God: Unique Aspects of the Passion Narrative in John." Pages 49–70 in *Behold the Lamb of God: The Fourth Annual BYU Religious Education Easter Conference*, edited by Richard Neitzel Holzapfel, Frank Judd Jr., & Thomas A. Wayment. Provo, Utah: The Religious Studies Center, 2008.

—. *The Miracles of Jesus.* Salt Lake City: Deseret Book, 2014.

—. *Worship: Adding Depth to Your Devotion.* Salt Lake City: Deseret Book, 2016.

Josephus. *The New Complete Works of Josephus.* Revised and expanded edition. Edited by Paul L. Maier. Translated by William Whiston. Grand Rapids, Michigan: Kregel, 1999.

Just, Roger. *Women in Athenian Law and Life.* New York: Routledge, 1989.

Keller, Roger G. "Mark and Luke: Two Facets of a Diamond." Pages 92–107 in *Sperry Symposium Classics: The New Testament,* edited by Frank F. Judd Jr., & Gaye Strathearn. Salt Lake City: Deseret Book, 2006.

Kimball, Spencer W. "Peter, My Brother." Pages 1–8 in *Speeches of the Year.* Provo: Brigham young University Press, 1971.

Koester, Craig R. "Theological Complexity and the Characterization of Nicodemus in John' Gospel." Pages 165–81 in *Characters and Characterization in the Gospel of John.* Edited by Christopher Skinner. Library of New Testament Studies 461. New York: Bloomsbury, 2013.

—. *Symbolism in the Fourth Gospel: Meaning, Mystery, and Community.* Minneapolis: Fortress Press, 2003.

Lee, Dorothy A. "Martha and Mary: Levels of Characterization in Luke and John." Pages 196–220 in *Characters and Characterization in the Gospel of John.* Edited by Christopher W. Skinner. Library of New Testament Studies 461. New York: Bloomsbury, 2013.

Longenecker, Richard N., ed. *Patterns of Discipleship in the New Testament.* Grand Rapids, Mich.: Eerdmans, 1996.

Mason, Patrick Q. *Planted: Belief and Belonging in an Age of Doubt.* Provo and Salt Lake City: Neal A. Maxwell Institute and Deseret Book, 2015.

Matson, Mark A. *In Dialogue with Another Gospel? The Influence of the Fourth Gospel on the Passion Narrative of the Gospel of Luke.* SBL Dissertation Series 178. Atlanta: Society of Biblical Literature, 2001.

Metzger, Bruce M. *A Textual Commentary of the Greek New Testament.* Second edition. Stuttgart: Deutsche Bibelgesellschaft, 1994.

Morris, Leon. *The Gospel according to John.* Revised. Grand Rapids, Mich.: Eerdmans, 1995.

O'Day, Gail R. *The Word Disclosed: Preaching the Gospel of John.* St. Louis: Chalice Press, 2002.

Parkin, Bonnie A. "Choosing Charity: The Good Part." *Ensign,* November 2003: 104–106.

Purvis, James D. "The Samaritan Problem: A Case Study in Jewish Sectarianism in the Roman Era." Pages 232–250 in *Traditions in Transformation: Turning Points in Biblical Faith.* Edited by Baruch Halpern and John D. Levenson. 1981.

Reid, Barbara A. *Choosing the Better Part: Women in the Gospel of Luke.* Collegeville, Minn.: The Liturgical Press, 1996.

Reinhartz, Adele. "The Gospel of John." Pages 561–600 in *A Feminist Commentary.* Edited by Elizabeth Schüssler Fiorenza. Vol. 2 of *Searching the Scriptures.* New York: Crossroad, 1994.

Roser, Nancy, Miriam Martinez, Charles Fuhrken, and Kathleen McDonnold. "Characters as Guides to Meaning." *The Reading Teacher* 60, no. 6 (2007): 548–59.

Schaberg, Jane. *The Resurrection of Mary Magdalene: Legends, Apocrypha, and the Christian Testament.* New York: Continuum, 2004.

Schnackenburg, Rudolph. *The Gospel according to John.* 3 vols. New York: Crossroad, 1990.

Schorch, Stefan. "The Origin of the Samaritan Community." *Linguistic and Oriental Studies from Poznan* 7 (2005): 7–16.

Seim, Turid Karlsen. "Role of Women in the Gospel of John." Pages 56–73 in *Aspects on the Johannine Literature.* Edited by Lars Hartman and Birger Olsson. Stockholm : Almqvist & Wiksell International, 1987.

Skinner, Christopher W. *Characters and Characterization in the Gospel of John.* New York: Bloomsbury T&T Clark, 2013.

—. *Reading John.* Eugene, Oreg.: Cascade Books, 2015.

Smith, Brian L. "The Witness of John." Pages 266–280 in *The Testimony of John the Beloved.* Salt Lake City: Deseret Book, 1998.

Smith, Julie M. "'She Hath Wrought a Good Work': The Anointing of Jesus in Mark's Gospel," *Studies in the Bible and Antiquity* 5 (2013): 31–46.

Szink, Terry L. and Frank F. Judd Jr. "John the Beloved in Latter-day Scripture (D&C 7)." Pages 90–107 in *The Doctrine and Covenants, Revelations in Context.* Edited by Andrew H. Hedges, J. Spencer Fluhman, and Alonzo L. Gaskill. Provo and Salt Lake City: Religious Studies Center, Brigham Young University, and Deseret Book, 2008.

Thompson, Marianne Meye. *John: A Commentary.* Louisville, Kent.: Westminster John Knox Press, 2015.

Top, Brent L. "Fallible but Faithful: How Simon the Fisherman Became Peter the Rock." Pages 1–12 in *The Ministry of Peter, the Chief Apostle.* The 43rd Annual Sidney B. Sperry Symposium. Edited by Eric D. Huntsman, and Shon D. Hopkin Frank F. Judd Jr. Provo and Salt Lake City: Religious Studies Center and Deseret Book, 2014.

Toplady, Augustus M. "Rock of Ages." No. 99 in *Sacred Songs No. 2.* Edited by J. McGranahan, G. Stebbins I. D. Sankey. New York: Biglow & Main Co., 1899.

Wilkins, M.J. "Disciples." Pages 176–182 in *Dictionary of Jesus and the Gospels.* Edited by Joel B. Green, & Scot McKnight. Downers Grove, Ill.: InterVarsity Press, 1992.

Williams, Ritva H. "The Mother of Jesus at Cana: A Social-Science Interpretation of John 2:1–12." *Catholic Biblical Quarterly* 59, no. 4 (1979): 679–92.

Index

H

I

J

About the Author

Eric Huntsman graduated from BYU in 1990 with a double major in Classical Greek and Latin. He then completed his MA and PhD in ancient history from the University of Pennsylvania. After teaching Classics at BYU from 1994 to 2003, he transferred to Religious Education, where he is a professor of Ancient Scripture. After teaching at the BYU Jerusalem Center from 2011–2012, he was appointed the coordinator of the Ancient Near Eastern Studies Program in the Kennedy Center for International Studies. He is scheduled to return to Jerusalem for a two-year appointment as the academic director of the Jerusalem Center program in 2020.

His teaching emphasis and scholarly work focuses on the New Testament Gospels, especially John. In addition to his academic publications, he has written a number of books for broader audiences, including *God So Loved the World*, *Good Tidings of Great Joy*, *The Miracles of Jesus*, and *Worship: Adding Depth to Your Devotion*. On August 7, 2018, he delivered a landmark BYU devotional address entitled, "Hard Sayings and Safe Spaces: Making Room for Struggle as Well as Faith." He has also been a frequent speaker with BYU Education Week, Women's Conference, and Deseret Book's Time Out for Women.

Dr. Huntsman served as a full-time missionary in the Thailand Bangkok Mission and as a bishop in Provo, Utah, for The Church of Jesus Christ of Latter-day Saints. He is currently an ordinance worker in the Provo Utah Temple and has been singing with the Mormon Tabernacle Choir since 2003. He and his wife, Elaine, are parents of two children, Rachel and Samuel.

Scan to visit

www.erichuntsman.com